The POGUES · THE LOST DECADE

Ann Scanlon

Omnibus Press
London/New York/Sydney/Cologne

Edited by **Chris Charlesworth**
Book Designed by **Giant**
Picture Research by **Ann Scanlon & Mary McCartney**
Project and typesetting co-ordinated by **Caroline Watson**

ISBN 0.7119.1471.0
Order No: OP44742

Exclusive distributors:

Book Sales Limited
8/9 Frith Street,
London W1V 5TZ, UK

Music Sales Corporation
24 East 22nd Street,
New York, NY 10010, USA

Music Sales Pty Limited
120 Rothschild Avenue,
Rosebery, NSW 2018, Australia

To the Music Trade only:
Music Sales Limited,
8/9 Frith Street,
London W1V 5TZ, UK

Picture credits:
Neil Anderson p11; Peter Anderson p21; 60/61, 69, 123 (top) &
124 (centre); Joe Bangay p36; Bleddyn Butcher p6, 28, 30, 64, 71,
75, 86, 89 & 108; Chris Clunn p15 & 52; Tom Collins p106/107,
110/111 & 123 (centre); Dead On Productions p22, 23, 31, 38, 39
& 56; Steve Double p12, 18, 43, 50, 65, 66, 67, 72, 97, 105, 113 &
117; London Features International p55 & 84; Stephen Mayes
p29 & 54; Renaud Monfourny p112; Clare Muller p83; Barry
Plummer p59; Steve Pyke p8, 19, 49, 85, 100, 102, 103, 104, 109,
118, 119, 120 (top & centre), 124 (top) & 127; Mary Scanlon
p16, 25, 41, 53, 74, 76, 77, 79, 80, 81, 82, 91, 92, 94, 98, 101 & 114;
Tom Sheehan p35 & 45; Paul Slattery p20, 27, 29, 33, 34, 37, 44, 47
& 62/63; Steve Tynan p40; Chris L. Urca p14; Richard Watts p4.

Typeset by Capital Setters, London.
Printed in England by Anchor Brendon Limited, Tiptree,
Essex.

Ann thanks her parents, Martin, Mary, Ant, Frank, Ferga, Jim
and Christine Mangan, Johanna and Alonso.

contents

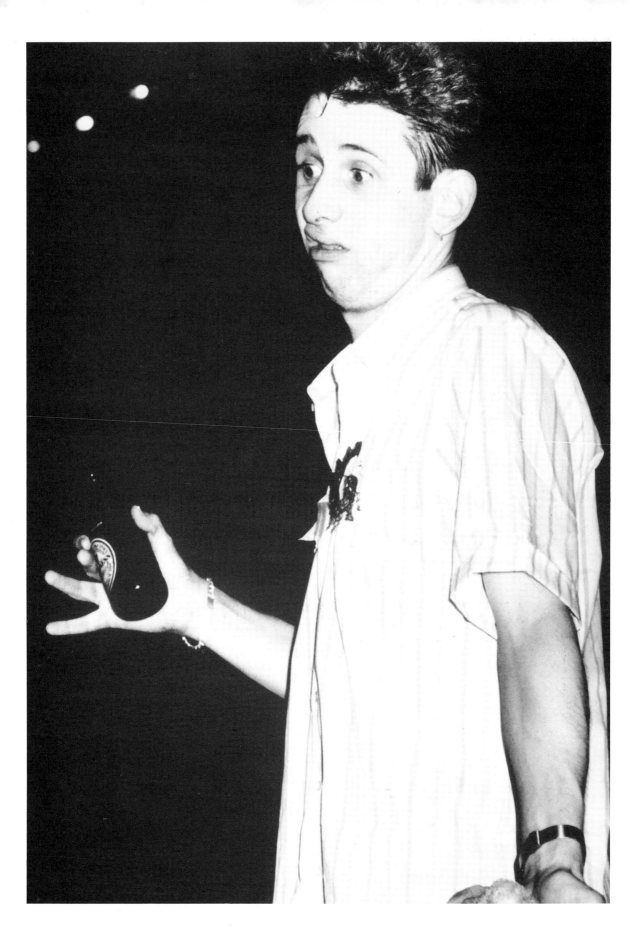

foreword

"There's all sorts of stories about us, and the myths are mixed up with the facts. Fellows would be telling me things that are supposed to have happened which didn't happen. All the good ones, you can't tell. You might offend somebody." RONNIE DREW (THE DUBLINERS)

the wayward way

Monday in autumn. London, King's Cross. Four scruffily besuited characters are gathered together in the front room of a tiny tenement flat. Musicians of sorts, they are setting out for their first ever collective appearance.

Just as they are about to leave the building, a fifth and final figure appears. Although his face is familiar, half the party haven't seen the stranger for some 18 months, and eyebrows are raised at his inappropriate apparel. Clad in black jeans, thug boots and a ripped leather jacket, he resembles a desperate hangover from 1977. He's welcomed all the same, and the five make their way down the street, round the corner and into a small saloon on the Gray's Inn Road.

Inside, the entourage hastily assemble a drum kit, unveil an accordion and dive for the bar. Three hours later, the establishment, now filled with 60 or so people, exudes the vague scent of inspired inebria. The band eventually stumble on stage, pick up their gear, pull up two mikes and it's "One, two, three, four . . ."

Pogue Mahone developed at a time when Irish music was neither profitable nor fashionable.

Easter 1981 and, as the charts glossed with Ultravox, Visage and Linx, it was impossible to escape the cheap sound of synthesizers and wholesale rumble of salsa. Shane MacGowan, proto-punk and face around town, had had his fill of London's gutless cocktail.

"There weren't any bands playing real music, emotional music that you could dance to or laugh to or cry to," he recalls. "It was either faggots with synthesizers, people buggering around with African music or wankers playing cranked out r 'n' b which had been going on for so long on the London pub scene that there wasn't anybody inspiring doing it any more."

Shane and his friend Jem Finer had lately joined a group that was going nowhere; he played bass and Jem guitar. They acted as backing band for a schoolteacher who wrote her own songs and whose relative affluence afforded the use of a studio for rehearsals. The drummer, Ollie, had an alter outlet known as The Millwall Chainsaws. The Chainsaws were a seldom-seen punk band fronted by Shane's long-time ally and soul-kick Spider Stacy.

Like Shane and Jem, The Chainsaws lived in Burton Street, King's Cross, and since they didn't have their own guitarist Shane often filled in; his singular three-chord stance perfectly suited their own. They also shared an increasing passion for Irish folk music.

"Shane would go round singing all this stuff and after a while I got used to him and started to know the words and tunes," says Spider. "And we'd go back to his place, drunk, and listen to Irish records that he'd borrowed off his dad or bought himself."

Their impromptu interpretation of Dubliners songs became a common sound in the north London pubs, but more often than not they were greeted with requests to leave.

One Monday that April, Shane and Ollie were down at Richard Strange's Cabaret Futura, a street-level poseurs' club frequented by the likes of Richard Jobson and the rising Soft Cell. Feeling the benefit of a night's drinking, Ollie marched up to Richard Strange and said: "Oi, Richard! We're in a band that plays Irish rebel songs – give us a gig here next week." Strange, ever keen to encourage individualism, immediately agreed. Two weeks later The New Republicans took to the boards.

Lining up as Ollie (drums), fellow Chainsaw Matt Jacobson (bass), a former New Bastard called John (guitar) and Shane (guitar, vocals) they blasted their way through a shambolic set; Spider, having lost his voice the day before, just stood on stage wondering who'd stolen his beer. Songs like 'The Patriot Game' and 'The Bold Fenian Men' were new to the raincoat-chic audience, but their reaction was favourable if uncertain. Upfront, the band provoked a more definite response.

"There was a group of about 20 drunken squaddies who took exception to the songs and started pelting us with chips," remembers Shane. "I don't think it was all that serious but it was reasonably alarming at the time." Spider remained oblivious to the hostility, but candidly admits, "I was so completely arseholed I wouldn't have known if they'd been throwing hand grenades." Eventually the management stepped in to pull the plugs on The New Republicans for the first and last time.

Thoroughly enjoying their performance and the instinctive crowd reaction, Shane was keen to turn the band into a going concern. The Chainsaws were renowned for their terminal apathy and only managed three skirmish-style rehearsals and a kitchen room demo over the next six months.

It was Jem Finer who shared MacGowan's enthusiasm. "In October of 1981 Shane was still warbling on about The New Republicans," says Jem. "So I asked him if he wanted someone else to play guitar and he said that he didn't know but he'd ask the others. Then a couple of months later he asked if I still wanted to play guitar, and a few weeks after that he invited me to his place to learn some songs. So everything took a remarkably long time."

By this stage, Shane was writing new material and the first original they attempted was 'Streams of Whiskey'. Inspired by the Celtic spirit of Brendan Behan and Flann O'Brien, the song was the ultimate in romantic impetuosity: 'I am going, I am going any which way the wind may be blowing/ I am going, I am going where streams of whiskey are flowing.' It summed up the free trade essence of Shane MacGowan.

When they had mastered a sufficient number of songs, they agreed that the best way to practise would be by busking. On several occasions they took their guitars to Finsbury Park tube station and played Irish, country and rock 'n' roll to indifferent travellers. "We weren't into the busking trip," says Shane. "We just did it for the money."

But their enterprise was less than viable. "Once we tried to go to Covent Garden and had an audition for the Piazza at 10 o'clock one morning," recalls Jem. "We played there for about half an hour with three people watching, one of which was a drunken Irishman who kept coming up to Shane and asking him to play 'Carrickfergus'. At the end of it the man from the Piazza sneered and said, 'Very few people have come here and failed what we like to call The Covent Garden Seal Of Quality. I'm sorry, you have failed.' I think it was at that point that we gave up busking."

In June 1982 they were ready to recruit a full line-up and auditioned a King's Cross neighbour, Andrew Ranken, on drums. Andrew clicked immediately, but he also sang in a cajun r 'n' b band, The Operation, and his loyalty lay with them. What's more, he was just about to go on a summer holiday which he wouldn't forfeit for anything.

A few weeks later, Dexys Midnight Runners had their third coming: with three-piece strings and evergreen washed-out dungarees, the Celtic sold ones unleashed the year's loudest refrain with 'Come On Eileen'.

"Suddenly there was all this press about Dexys and all that Celtic thing and it just seemed like a really bizarre coincidence," says Jem.

"We just thought these blokes had come up with a watered down version of what we were doing," says Shane. "We thought they should have stuck to soul which they were good at."

Towards the end of the summer, while MacGowan and Finer sought an accordion player, Shane remembered that a former flat-mate, James Fearnley, could play piano. Jem consequently turned up on James' doorstep, presented him with an accordion, and said, "We thought if anyone would be able to play this, it would be you."

Taken aback, James was less than convinced about the band. "I'd never played accordion before, and I didn't really go a bundle on the idea. I thought that it would just be another folk group."

Nevertheless, he agreed to give it a go and spent September rehearsing with Shane and Jem; they showed him the songs and he learnt to play accordion to them. Meanwhile, 'Country' Jem had swapped his guitar for a banjo, an instrument which was equally foreign to him. "The way that I learnt was entirely influenced by trying to play Irish music in a country style of banjo playing," he says.

By this time, John Hasler had been roped in on drums and, less than a month after James and Jem first picked up the accordion and banjo, MacGowan and Finer asked Justin and Vicki Ward to give them a date at The Pindar Of Wakefield in King's Cross. The band was duly booked for October 4, 1982.

Three nights before the big event Shane telephoned Spider Stacy to tell him that – 18 months on from The New Republicans – they had another gig. But by the eve of their début they had yet to come up with a suitable name. Among the suggestions were The Men They Couldn't Hang and The Noisy Boysies, but they couldn't agree on either. Sitting in a pub that night, Spider suggested to Shane that they should christen themselves 'Pogue Mahone' elementary Gaelic for 'Kiss my arse'. The name stuck, and Pogue Mahone it was.

9

Shane MacGowan was born in Kent, on Christmas Day 1957, but his childhood passed in his mother's Tipperary home, not far from Nenagh and the call of the rippling Shannon.

His mother, Therese, came from a typical Irish family: the rare auld stock. Her father had died when she was three so she grew up in her grandparents' farmhouse, which housed a huge family of 14 people and, although there wasn't much money, their home was rich in music, dancing and the Gaelic tongue.

Therese was a talented singer and traditional Irish dancer. She commanded an extensive range of songs and regularly won prizes at fleadh-ceoils, the music festivals which were a characteristic part of country life. She was also exceptionally handsome and it wasn't long before she was drawn to the bright lights of Dublin, where her raging beauty quickly secured a modelling career.

It was in the city that she met and married Maurice MacGowan, who came from a middle class but not affluent Dublin family. He was a literate man forever reading and writing, and particularly keen on poetry, and although his voice was no match for Therese's he shared her love of music. His taste ranged from jazz and blues through the country sounds of Hank Williams and Johnny Cash to old Dublin ballads like 'Waxies Dargle'.

Liking Irish music was, says Shane, as natural as liking the sound of his mother's voice. "When I was really little, I was brought up by the people in Tipperary who knew millions of songs. It was real gut-level stuff, music that's been handed down from generation to generation."

There were a dozen people living in the family farmhouse, and almost every night the neighbours would gather in to sing and play traditional music. "Listening to and singing Irish music was a part of life. I had an auntie who played concertina, an uncle who played accordion, cousins who played banjo and tin whistle. So it's perfectly natural for me to sing Irish songs, I've been doing it since I was a kid and the feel of it is no problem. It was something I never thought about."

When he was six, Shane's parents took him to England, and he and his younger sister, Siobhan, were brought up in central London. "Even at that age, it was a sharp contrast from the country in Ireland. I used to know bits of Gaelic because my mother speaks it fluently, but once I hit the city I forgot it; I became immersed in the society of London. On the other hand, because there's an Irish scene in London you never forget the fact that you originally came from Ireland. There are lots of Irish pubs, so there was always Irish music in bars and on jukeboxes. I had an uncle who ran a pub in Dagenham, and I stayed there a lot of the time. Then every summer I would spend my school holidays back in Tipp."

Besides an inherent love for Irish music and the blues, Shane went through the usual pop phase. "In my early teens I liked heavy metal, which was good, but you soon get sick of it. Then when I started going to discos I got heavily into soul and reggae."

He was a brilliant scholar and at 14, his flair for poetry and prose secured him a place at Westminster. But instead of flourishing in a top public school, he "just buggered around and got kicked out after one year." He spent numerous teenage hours wandering around Piccadilly but, unlike so many rootless kids, Shane was never too far from home.

When he left school, he worked as everything from being a shelver in a supermarket to a porter at the Indian Embassy. At the same time England was being blitzed by economic recession and, before long, the children of Boom, Beatles and Backing Britain were bristling with anger, frustration and sheer Boredom.

At 18, MacGowan became a barman in The Griffin Tavern, Charing Cross, and a regular on London's pub-rock scene where he witnessed the likes of the anarchic Pink Fairies and blistering r 'n' b from the 101ers and Dr Feelgood.

Nips Shane MacGowan and James Fearnley, December 1979

Shane MacGowan

On June 15 1976, while waiting for the 101ers, he encountered The Sex Pistols. Already infatuated with the glam narcissism of The New York Dolls, the Pistols blew him away. Their searing energy and frozen nonchalance epitomized the disaffection of a generation.

"Seeing The Sex Pistols changed my life – it changed loads of people's lives. There was a band that just got up there and made a really horrible noise and didn't give a shit. They were all our age and had dyed hair and wore brothel creepers, and it was just a question of, 'Yeah, Fuck it. I hate everything and they're actually doing it.' I thought they were brilliant; the best group I've ever seen."

Shane chopped off his hair, jacked in his job and watched the world turn dayglo. For 12 breakneck months there was action, excitement and round-the-clock kicks.

"The whole scene was based on gigs at places like the ICA and going to nightclubs that stayed open all night, taking loads of speed and drinking Pernod – as opposed to going out to a disco with your mates, drinking beer, getting in fights and picking up some bird. The punk scene was completely asexual so you'd get both sexes hanging around together, not doing anything except staying out all night and dancing. Like the best place going at the start was Louise's, which was originally a lesbian club in Soho; that was the first really good nightclub.

"One thing that's got to be pointed out about the original punk scene, though, is that it was extremely élitist, like mod in the early sixties. The whole thing was basically created by the beginning of 1977 and anyone who got into it after that was just a pile of shit, in terms of the way that people thought. Half of it was working class disco kids and the other half was art students, there was a genuine working class thing in it – that's why it got so big in the end – but it was the hip working class.

"Initially it was all about style and about fuck, literally fuck everything, 'Fuck it – I don't care. I don't care if they drop the bomb, I'm still going down to Louise's in my new pink brothel creepers.' But it was incredibly élitist: if you walked into a club wearing the wrong thing you'd be laughed out of the place; you'd have to leave the country!"

In October of 1976, a girl called Jane (later to reappear as a Modette) turned Shane into a mini-legend. "I was up the front at this Clash gig in the ICA, and me and this girl were having a laugh, which involved biting each other's arms 'till they were completely covered in blood and then smashing up a couple of bottles and cutting each other up a bit. Anyway, in the end she went a bit over the top and bottled me in the side of the head. Gallons of blood came out and someone took a photograph. I never got it bitten off – although we had bitten each other to bits – it was just a heavy cut.

"But I got into *The Evening Standard* and that made me a 'face' from then on. People used to stop me in the street and say, 'You're the guy who had his ear bitten off, you're great man.' 'Cos that's what it turned into. It's like the old story about the bloke who catches the fish, he says that it weighs this much and it's that big and within a couple of day's it's a whale."

Shane O'Hooligan was ubiquitous: behind the reputed Rock On record stall in Soho Market by day and up front at every gig by night. Struck by the vibrant honesty of The Jam, he swore to their importance when he created his own one-off fanzine, *Bondage*. He quickly formed a group with his friend Shanne Bradley, and it was she who named them Nipple Erectors.

On December 1, 1976, The Pistols swore at Bill Grundy on tea-time TV, and punk went provocatively public. By the time it had been neutered and mass produced enough for the King's Road tourists, punk was over.

"It started as an expression of orginality," says Shane, "but within a year people were getting into it as a kind of cattle movement. Like loads and loads of punks crowding into halls to see The Ramones or Clash. I'm not knocking those people but the whole point was to be yourself; a complete individual.

"Speaking as one of the great trendsetters of the movement," he laughs, "the minute that anybody turned up looking a bit like you then you'd change. But in the end there were loads of people walking around with anarchist signs and hair spiked out dyed green, and wearing leather jackets, Doc Martens and jeans, just like Sid."

The Nipple Erectors immortalized their distinctive rockabilly clout on 'King Of The Bop'/ 'Nervous Wreck'. The single was produced by Stan Brennan, Shane's employer in the Soho record store Rocks Off, and the band attracted a considerable amount of attention before shortening their name to the less controversial Nips.

"We were a no bullshit group. We just used to get up, whatever state we were in, and without all the posing that a lot of other people did. We never gave all this 'I'm An Artist' shit; we were always in touch with the audience. It sounds corny but it's true."

The Nips built up a loyal following on the London circuit and issued three singles 'All The Time In The World', the notable pop ballad 'Gabrielle' and the Paul Weller-produced 'Happy Song'/'Nobody To Love'. They also recorded a live LP, casually titled 'Only The End Of The Beginning'.

They had a legendary reputation for line-up changes and, by the time they disbanded, had been through four guitarists and more drummers than anyone cares to remember. "The only people who were in The Nips from the beginning to the end were me and Shanne. The rest of them lasted as long as they lasted and then we kicked them out. It wasn't set out like that but that's the way things happened. In the end we had a really good group – James Fearnley was the guitarist – and we didn't break up properly 'till the end of 1980."

With the calm borne of perspective, Shane says of punk: "It wasn't a revolution like everyone makes out; it was just a change of style. At the time we thought, 'This is it, we've got it sussed,' but we were just a bunch of teenagers and the dreams disappeared like smoke out of an opium pipe. So at the end of the day you were left with a load of old brothel creepers, a lot of hair gel, a couple of bottles of crazy colour and the dole. That happened to loads of people, some got out of it and others didn't. Lots of people I know from that time are dead and I just happen to be one of the lucky ones at the moment.

"But," he states, "it was the best thing that ever happened to me, it completely changed my life at a really important stage. If it hadn't been for punk, I'd probably be some drunken shithead barman running my own pub."

After the brief excitement of the 2-Tone ska movement, Shane's interest in the club scene was temporarily revived by the celebrated dance world of Blitz and Spandau Ballet.

"The whole thing was about making the band part of the atmosphere, which could only work on a small level in London. It was a hip élitist scene which was a bit like punk. In fact, I'd known all the people who were involved in that club scene from the punk days; it was the same crowd.

"I thought that Spandau Ballet were a great band whenever I saw them – which was only two or three times, because they only played live about six times before they had a hit record. So for a while, because I wasn't doing anything else, I got into that. But it soon tapered off, and then the whole scene went down. It was appalling."

It was at this point that Shane MacGowan was drawn back to his Irish folk roots. "The music that I felt naturally emotionally involved with."

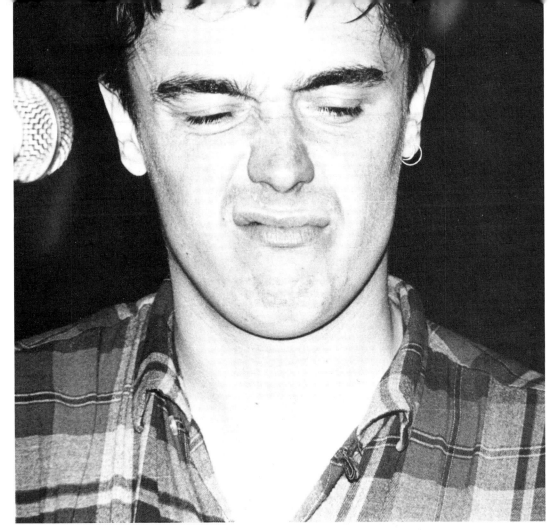

Spider Stacy

Although he was born in Eastbourne, on December 14 1958, Peter Stacy's childhood was coloured by foreign shores.

When he was two, his father's work forced the family to move to British Guyana, on the north east coast of South America. After six months the Stacys returned to the Sussex coast but then, in 1964, the lure of oil took them to Libya for two and a half years. Back in Eastbourne again, his parents separated and Peter stayed with his mother who took a job in Surrey and, a few months later, in Berkshire.

"My mum was assistant matron at this boarding school called Big Shot, near Broadmoor, so that's where I went to school. Then she left half way through the term and I had to stay there without her; I hated it. When I finished we moved to London, where she met up with my dad again and we've lived there ever since."

When Peter was 12 a girl friend rechristened him Spider, in recognition of his angular body and liquorice legs. He had already established a marked preference for The Rolling Stones over the more popular Beatles. "I didn't like the idea of The Beatles, I thought they were wimps. I always preferred The Stones 'cos they had that darkness and hardness about them."

Stacy confirmed himself as the hippest kid on the block by being the first to get into The Velvet Underground and, later, The Stooges. "I used to listen to all kinds of music: around 1972 I liked T Rex, Gary Glitter and Roxy Music. And – for some reason, I can't figure out why now – I really used to like Genesis and Pink Floyd. But," he quickly adds, "I never liked Yes and I never liked ELP." His favourite records included The Faces' 'A Nod's As Good As A Wink To A Blind Horse' and Humble Pie's live version of 'Hallelujah', "It goes on for about 15 minutes, it's so excrutiatingly boring it's brilliant." He also displayed the usual mid-seventies tendency for Led Zeppelin, Deep Purple and Black Sabbath.

In 1975, aged 16, Spider was expelled from school. He spent the next year doing a series of dead-end jobs. "The first job I had was working in a car wash, that was good, I liked it. Then I worked in an electrical warehouse, shelved in a supermarket and did all sorts of crap like that."

He was equally non-plussed by the stale music scene. "It sounds like a cliché, but it was all so *boring*, there was just nothing to get excited about. Then, sometime in '76, I saw Dr Feelgood and I thought they were brilliant. They were hardly revolutionary but they were really exciting. And then, a couple of nights later, I was at some party and someone put on 'Blitzkrieg Bop', and I wondered, 'What the fuck is this?' I'd heard of The Ramones and thought they were Puerto Ricans, so I got a real shock when I picked up the album cover and saw all these white guys with long hair when I had imagined these real sharp Puerto Rican kids with DAs and quiffs. But I thought 'Blitzkrieg Bop' was brilliant, and knew something was definitely going on."

Not long afterwards Spider was watching Bill Grundy's *Today* programme and, like thousands, he was struck by the 'Filth and Fury' of The Sex Pistols. "I saw The Pistols and that was it. Everything fell into place and made sense. The next day I went out to try and buy 'Anarchy In The UK' but couldn't because everyone had bought it before me. So I bought 'Stupidity' instead and managed to steal a copy of 'Anarchy' off someone who didn't realize what it was all about."

He started going down to The Roxy, in Covent Garden, a squalid showcase for the new bands and, until April 1977, punk's premier home. He also joined The New Bastards. "These mates of mine had started a band in mid '76 called The Bastards, but I'd lost touch with them. Then we met up again through going to the same gigs, and they reformed calling themselves the New Bastards. I was the drummer . . . I play drums even worse than I sing."

The band's initial engagement was at a notorious comprehensive school in Brent. Hell-bent on hedonism, The New Bastards singer passed the pre-gig hour downing 16 cans of Harp Lager, and the only song that he could remember, as he was carried from the toilets to the stage, was Stacy's Pulitzer special 'Filthy': 'God you smell, you really reek/ You better have a bath this week/ You don't even wash your clothes/ You've got scum between your toes/ 'Cos you're filthy.'

They had to repeat it six times. Suitably inspired, Spider Stacy resolved to form The Millwall Chainsaws with two characters of similar disposition, Ollie Watts and Matt Jacobson. "We started talking about it in '77, but we were all so indolent and drunk and stoned the whole time that it took us two years to get round to actually doing it."

Meanwhile, Spider found temporary employment in filling stations, and somehow ended up as a car salesman. "I was quite good at flogging cars, only I can't drive which is a bit of a handicap. Also I used to go to work in a black suit wearing a black shirt and tie, and my hair was Throbbing Gristle batch. Well 'ard," he laughs.

On New Years Day, 1979, The Millwall Chainsaws took to the stage in style. They opened for The North London Invaders (later to become Madness) at the Film Makers' Co-op in Camden Town. Appearing as Spider shouting, Ollie occa-

sionally hitting drums and Matt booming in on bass, The Chainsaws had their finest moment with the Stacy penned 'Skinhead Escapes'. Drawn from Richard Allen's Skinhead series, it was a bootboy smoocher which began: 'Joe Hawkins died for somebody's sins, not mine/ I'm buggered if I'm gonna pay this fine, one, two, three, four/ Me mother says wanking makes you blind/ The teacher says I ain't got no mind/ Bricks and mortar make me whine/ Skinhead escapes over the wall/ Skinhead escapes over the wall.'

"That was one of our best gigs," remembers Spider. "We also did a song called 'Fuck Off' which consisted of the, er, musicians going, 'BOOM! BOOM!' and me shouting, 'Fuck Off! Fuck Off!' and rolling around on the floor and generally making an exhibition of myself."

Delighted by their début, The Chainsaws agreed to go ahead with a full scale tour of London. They upgraded their act to the extent of learning two more songs and were known to do an impressive version of 'No Fun'.

In the spring of 1978, the band moved to King's Cross where they became itinerant residents of Burton Street. Living on the same street was Shane MacGowan (whom Spider had first encountered 12 months earlier in the Roundhouse urinal at a Ramones gig) and it wasn't long before MacGowan had been adopted into the Chainsaw ranks.

"For the kind of stuff we were doing Shane was *perfect*," enthuses Stacy. "He knew exactly what was required. Technically he's not a good guitarist but in terms of feel and energy he's brilliant."

Early in 1981, The Millwall Chainsaws completed their first tour of London and, inspired by The Dubliners, temporarily emerged as The New Republicans.

"The Chainsaws did seven gigs in the space of two years. But it was better than being pressurized," says Spider. "We've never split up. It was just a long time between gigs."

17

Jem Finer

teenage takeover of the early sixties. "I was brought up on The Beatles, Rolling Stones, the normal *Ready Steady Go* sort of fodder; Elvis Presley and Tamla Motown. When I was 12 everyone in school was really into Northern Soul discos. Then, at 13, I started going to see any band that came along. I saw lots of crap and some really good ones, like Deep Purple. I also used to go to pop festivals and saw loads of good groups, like The Doors and Jimi Hendrix at the Isle of Wight."

Jem was introduced to country music via The Grateful Dead's folk-rock and, later, the tough trucking tales of Commander Cody. "I used to listen to them and then I got interested in hearing the originals. Half the time it used to make me laugh rather than actually liking the music. I mean, a lot of country music is funny because the singers think they're serious. But there's some really brilliant stuff too, and Hank Williams is one of the best."

His favourite contemporary band was The Faces. By 1971 their raucous sets, usually lubricated by vast quantities of alcohol, were among the finest live shows in the country; and they attracted a fanatical following. "The Faces were the band that I used to go and see whenever I could. I never followed them round but they used to play quite a lot in Manchester. They always used to look like they were really enjoying themselves, half pissed, there was something that got to you whether they were good or bad. When they were good they were brilliant and quite often they were really bad. But there was just a feeling that you got. It was like being at a football match."

Not surprisingly, Jem was a regular at Old Trafford in the days of glory, glory and Sir Matt Busby. "I used to go to see Manchester United when they were really, really brilliant. When they had George Best, Bobby Charlton and Dennis Law. There was about three seasons when I went to all the home matches and a lot of away ones too."

Born in Stoke-on-Trent, on July 20 1955, Jem Finer grew up in the Staffordshire town of Keele. When he was 10 his family moved closer to Manchester, and settled in Knutsford.

He developed an appetite for music in the

At 18, he went to Keele University to study Computing and Sociology. Having completed his course in 1977, he worked on a barge in the South of France then travelled around for a year before settling in London. "I was always a bit like a displaced Londoner," he maintains. "Both my parents are from London and we used to go there to visit the family. It wasn't my fault I had to live in Knutsford and Keele."

In the city, Jem found work in an office, a warehouse and, for a while, an adventure playground. "Then I got really fed up with everything and decided I was going to live abroad. So I did a month's course teaching English as a foreign language and was going to go to Italy. But immediately afterwards I got a job teaching photography to delinquents on a scheme called Intermediate Treatment In Deptford."

Throughout this period, Finer lived in number 32, Burton Street, a house which he sometimes shared with Spider Stacy and, later, Shane MacGowan. "There were lots of bands in Burton Street," says Jem. "There was this group called Charge – a sort of anarcho punk band who played benefits all over the place – and they had this basement done out like a rehearsal room, so there was always people just messing around with instruments."

Among the many bands who frequented Burton Street were a psychotic r 'n' b combo known as The Petals. One day, their bassist failed to show up so Jem stepped in and instantly became a permanent fixture. "I don't think The Petals were ever destined for great things. We were ragged round the edges and not entirely serious."

By 1980 The Petals had petered out. But, following the break up of The Nips, Finer and MacGowan started rehearsing together, and eventually laid the foundations for the prototype Pogue Mahone.

James Thirkhill Fearnley was born on October 9 1954, in Worsley, West Manchester. At the age of 11 he went, in family tradition, to Ackworth Friends School near Wakefield, where he excelled as a choir treble. He was 16 before his voice broke.

During his first year at Ackworth, James took piano lessons. "It was the first instrument I'd ever played, but the teacher was so horrible that after a year and a half I wanted to pack it in. I'd turn up to lessons with bandages around my hands saying that a window had dropped on them, and it just so happened that the fellow before me had done exactly the same thing – so the teacher didn't believe either of us."

Fearnley was eventually excused piano lessons and, when himself and two school friends decided to form their own band, his parents bought him a Spanish guitar. His taste in music was, at this stage, dominated by Motown, The Rolling Stones and white blues. "I got to know a lot of riffs on guitar but they were learnt second hand off white blues guitarists like Peter Green and Eric Clapton. The only gigs that I went to from school were Cream and Bowie."

James took a degree in Humanities at Ealing Technical College and after leaving college, in September 1977, he decided to live in Germany and hit Berlin during the peak of Baader Meinhof activity. He took his guitar with him and soon met up with another musician. "I played with this black lad in a couple of clubs in Berlin. He was a singer/songwriter and wanted someone to borrow money off and help out with a few songs. He was really good on his own, and I only played on a couple of numbers. I lent him some money and I never saw him again, but he said that I was okay on guitar and I ought to get myself into a group. So I came back to England with the intention of playing."

Back home, a singer called Nick Wade (later Nik of Alien Sex Fiend) had advertised for a guitarist. Fearnley joined the band, but the un-christened outfit only made one demo before

splitting for good.

Later he had a brief affair with The Mixers, playing several times around the Kingston and Richmond area, but directly afterwards he met up with The Nips.

"I had an audition and said, 'I'm not going to join the group unless you can give me somewhere to live.' And that's how I ended up in this squat – or so I thought it was – with Jem, Shane and various other people in King's Cross."

The last edition of The Nips consisted of James, Shane, Shanne Bradley and Jon Moss. "Jon Moss is a brilliant drummer, and a great bloke – although he wouldn't sing 'The Holly And The Ivy' when we played with The Jam at The Music Machine. We were all dressed in women's night-dresses and Jon was wearing a pair of frilly pants and wouldn't come out to the front of the stage to do backing vocals."

At the end of 1980 The Nips finally called it a day. Simultaneously, their Burton Street home was designated a dangerous building, so the Housing Association moved James to alternative accommodation in Mornington Crescent. It was then that he joined a soul band, The Giants.

"We had a great singer called Paul Cox. He's got a really good soul voice for a white fellow, and I think he's got his own band together now. The Giants were a good group for me to be in 'cos most of the stuff I played before was thrashing. But by playing soul I just came up with these half learnt Steve Cropper guitar licks, and the rest of it was made up. I really enjoyed playing soul guitar, but that group split up too."

On the demise of The Giants, James decided to hang up his guitar and turn instead to writing. Diversion came when Jon Moss who had joined a group known as Culture Club, paid a visit.

"He came round to my flat, and asked me to listen to a tape 'cos they were looking for a guitarist. We were sitting in his car, with no lights on, listening to this tape and Jon Moss was tapping his feet so that the whole car was shaking. You can

James Fearnley

imagine what it must have looked like, coming down Arlington Road and seeing these two fellows in a car that's going up and down! Anyway, I told him that I could easily play what was on the tape, and he said if he didn't ring me I should call him. But neither of us phoned, and Culture Club got famous directly afterwards."

After that, James sold his Telecaster replica, and spent the next year writing. He turned out a play and a short story (their topics wildly veering from illness and old age to straight sex) and a series of short pieces. "I wrote for four hours every morning. I did that religiously, weekends as well."

Mid 1982, and Fearnley had more or less forgotten about playing in bands when Jem Finer, and friend, paid him an unexpected visit.

'. . . Last night as I slept, I dreamt I met with Behan,' Shane MacGowan belted his way through the joyous strains of 'Streams of Whiskey', while Spider Stacy yelled and screamed, belched and sneered and generally behaved at outrageous odds with the others.

The set itself was a shambling collection of Dubliners favourites and loosely practised originals. From the hazardous instrumental clang of 'The Clobberer' and 'Connemara Let's Go', through 'Dark Streets Of London' to the soulful strains of 'Peggy Gordon' and the plaintive cry of Brendan Behan's 'The Auld Triangle'.

The Pindar crowd had already sensed that this was the beginning of something special when the band played 'Waltzing Matilda': a version so moving that even the obnoxious Stacy was reduced to tears. "The refrain at the end hit an emotional nerve," he says, "and I just started crying. It was really embarrassing."

More embarrassed, however, were Jem and James who found Stacy's Chainsaw behaviour, not to mention his sartorial garb, unforgiveable. "We went down really well," says Jem, "and everybody said it was brilliant – which it wasn't, although obviously there was something there – but you want to get rid of that bloke. He's a complete arsehole."

MacGowan, though, was anxious for Spider to remain in the band, and it was privately agreed that Stacy would borrow an old suit, get a grip on his volume control and learn to play the tin whistle.

The next day, Shane was wandering down Oxford Street when he bumped into Cait O'Riordan. Cait had been invited to the Pindar, but it was the day before her dole cheque, and she didn't have the money to get home to Queens Park. Now, with a freshly cashed giro in her hand, it seemed like a good idea to go for a drink.

While London woke up to punk, 11-year-old Caitlin O'Riordan was doing her homework and in bed by 10.00 pm.

She was born in Nigeria, on January 4 1965, of Celtic blood; her father came from Clare and her mother Musselburgh, near Edinburgh. But before she was two, civil war persuaded the O'Riordans to leave Africa and head for London.

Caitlin grew up to the sound of country and western and Radio 2. "Before I got my first radio, I just liked what was played on Radio 2, really calm, middle-of-the-road stuff; and my dad had cheap Johnny Cash records and The Dubliners albums. Then every Sunday we used to go to the Irish Club in Teddington which had an Irish jukebox. I liked that stuff as well, 'cos I associated those records with my packet of crisps and lemonade on a Sunday."

When she was 14, she broadened her musical horizon. "I got a radio and started listening to all the John Peel shows when I went to bed." It was while listening to Peel that Cait was struck by a song titled 'Gabrielle'. She went to buy it from Rocks Off Records, and working behind the counter was The Nips singer Shane MacGowan. "It's all really cosmic," she smiles, "a series of coincidences, both good and bad."

Later Cait acquired a black bass guitar. "I didn't learn to play it, I just had it because it was

Cait O'Riordan with Shane MacGowan

beautiful. It was a mean, punk, cheap bass which I kept under my bed."

Her introduction to live music came courtesy of Orange Juice and Postcard Pop. "The emergence of Postcard records coincided with me just coming up to 16 – before ever being allowed out of the house – so I went to all those gigs."

But by autumn 1982, Postcard was fizzling and the music scene looked limited.

Sitting in The Hog In The Pound, South Molton Street, Shane talked about the gig and Cait casually mentioned she had a bass guitar. Suitably soused, Shane saw O'Riordan as the perfect solution to Pogue Mahone's basslessness.

"Full of my whiskey and my giro, he said, 'You're in the band'," recalls Cait. "I went hungry all that next week."

Already acquainted with Spider, Cait was introduced to James, Jem and John in the pub, before her first rehearsal. James shook her hand and said,

"You must be Cait, the new bass player." She replied, "No, I'm just Cait." There would be no illusions.

She made her debut on October 23, when they headlined for King Kurt at Clapham's 101 Club. By going on early, King Kurt could get legless later but, as a result, Pogue Mahone played to a drastically diminished crowd of 20. They also had to wade their way through King Kurt's token trail of talcum powder, flowers and rabbit offal.

"It was absolutely disgusting," says Jem. "The stage was covered in goo so that every step you took you stuck to the floor. I trod on this thing that squelched and flew out from under my foot. I looked down and it was a rabbit's kidney, and there was a rabbit's head just lying there. Revolting."

While Cait sat on a stool, carefully strumming on Jem's Monkee-sized old bass, Spider was bashing his brains out by way of percussion. "That

23

was the first time that I employed the beer tray," he says. "I woke up the next morning with a knee that was turning black, 'cos I was banging it on my knee as well as my head, and my forehead had gone green. Actually, it looked quite fetching."

A couple of weeks later, they trooped round to Justin Ward's flat, and recorded a demo on his four-track studio. "We did 'Waltzing Matilda', 'Poor Paddy' and 'Streams Of Whiskey'," says Jem. "But it was really unfortunate, because when we copied it on to tape only one side of the cassette was working. So you could hardly hear the bass and drums, and it came out sounding really folky."

Billing themselves as The Black Velvet Underground, the Pogues' next outing was to the 100 Club on Oxford Street where they supported The Milkshakes and The Sting-rays. Their short, spirited set was perfectly attuned to the psychotic tendencies of the gathering, and the wreckin' crew went crazy.

"All I remember was John's drum kit falling off the stage," says Spider. "It was probably trying to get away from him and find someone who could hit it properly."

Spider had, meanwhile, cemented his own position by making a start on the tin whistle. "I found it easier than I thought I would," he says. "It's a good instrument to pick out a simple tune on, the fingering is very logical and straightforward. I got this book which had diagrams of the finger movements for tunes like 'Amazing Grace' and 'Silent Night'. And from the very first day I was able to play 'Silent Night', which gave me the encouragement to push on."

By December it had become clear that if Pogue Mahone were going anywhere, then John Hasler wouldn't be with them. It was left to Jem and Cait to issue the forthright suggestion that he should try harder, or they would find someone else. Jumping before he was pushed, Hasler quit the band.

Finding a decent replacement proved difficult, and Pogue Mahone entered 1983 with an all-time

low at Camden's Dingwalls. They were drunk and disorganised to the point of total collapse while the 'drummer' – who had been recruited only hours before – made John Hasler look like Art Blakey.

In the crowd that night was Philip Chevron. A former Radiator From Space and, at the time, working in Camden's Rock On record shop, Chevron had come with a curiosity fuelled by acquaintance. He wasn't exactly swept off his feet. "I thought they were dreadful," he says. "But there was the knowledge that if they could get it right and sort out the line-up then they would work a treat." Chevron resolved not to watch them again for a few months.

"Dingwalls was the last time we were really bad," says James. "Jem was so frustrated that he started banging his head against the dressing room wall."

Their subsequent dates saw a string of haphazard drummers and equally erratic sized crowds: one week they'd be playing to 70, the next to a dozen. Most of their gigs took place at The Pindar Of Wakefield as part of a series of nights run by two sisters called Fiona and Gerri Murray, and titled Hey Wire.

Among 10 people watching Pogue Mahone at the Pindar, one night that February, was Darryl Hunt, a drinking acquaintance of Jem Finer and a regular on the King's Cross scene. "They were just another of the many groups playing at the Pindar who all seemed to know each other," he says. "But they were really good, really good fun."

By this time, Shane and Jem had decided that their problem was not just with a drummer, but with the drums themselves. They quickly created their own sound: based on a unique two-piece 'kit' of floor tom-tom and snare drum. "We just worked out what we wanted the drums to sound like, and made a tape," says Jem. "Then we gave it round to various people."

Among these was their original choice, Andrew Ranken.

Andrew Ranken

25

Born in London's Ladbroke Grove, on November 13 1953, Andrew Ranken's earliest memory is the sound of steam trains rattling to and fro into Paddington Station.

"When I was two years old my father used to take me to meet my older sister from school. We used to cross a bridge which went over all the railway tracks, and he would put me on his shoulders so that I could see over the parapet. In those days it was steam trains, and because it's a big terminus there were lots of them. I was really excited just by the sound of the trains and the smoke."

There was always music in the Ranken household. The radio was permanently on, and the first tunes to make an impression on Andrew were the themes from *Music While You Work* and *The Archers*. His parents were keen on Gilbert and Sullivan, and their sizeable collection of records included Benny Goodman, Glenn Miller and Artie Shaw.

When Andrew was six, the family moved to a small town in Sussex where they lived throughout the sixties. The first record that he bought was 'She Loves You' by The Beatles.

"For a long time it was The Beatles and The Rolling Stones. They were just the best two groups in the world as far as I could make out. Then when I was about 14 I started looking at the inside of record labels, where it says who wrote the songs, and there were all these names of people that I'd never heard of. It was then I became aware that it wasn't just English pop music, and that it actually came from somewhere else which was rhythm and blues."

During this period, 1967/68, England witnessed a blues boom with new bands like Fleetwood Mac, Chicken Shack and Savoy Brown. "I went for it in a big way, and I've loved r 'n' b ever since. There were bands like the original Fleetwood Mac who were a straight blues band, and a really good one as well, doing cover versions of people that they really admired and The Rolling Stones were doing

that too. It took white bands to reinterpret what people like Muddy Waters and Bobby Bland had done to actually get it across to a wide enough audience for anyone to be able to make any money out of it. But if those guys hadn't been there then popular music wouldn't be like it is, and it's really sick that they never reaped the rewards they should have."

At 14, Andrew was enthused enough to start playing the drums. He was also given a taste for Irish music when he paid his first visit to his father's Ballyneety birthplace, a small village just south of Limerick. "I got on really well with my grandfather," he remembers, "he used to sing to me."

When he left school, Andrew went to art college in London and made up for lost time by going to Ronnie Scott's more often than he could afford. "It was comparatively cheap to get in upstairs, and then I'd sneak downstairs. I saw lots of different people and got quite into jazz. It was partly things like Benny Goodman, which I like although I prefer the be-bop stuff."

One of the first performers he saw at Ronnie Scott's was Elvin Jones. "The first time I heard him it was so exciting. I just thought, 'Yeah, this is it', and I still do. I don't have favourite musicians but as far as drummers go I think he's in a class of his own. Lots of people cite him as an influence, but there's nobody who plays like him. It's just really interesting, mentally, to try and work out what he's doing. Technique can be learnt, but it's the way he interprets things and, to me, that's what it's all about. He's completely brilliant, and I've been watching him for years."

During his foundation period at art school, Andrew was the drummer in Lola Cobra, a band fronted by a girl called Lene Lovich. But after a year of college conformism he decided to abandon art and hitch-hike around Europe instead. He sold his drums to raise the fare to Holland but on arriving in Amsterdam had all his money and possessions stolen. The Ranken losses were recup-

erated by working for eight weeks in a peanut factory, and he spent a further seven months in France and Italy.

Back in London, a friend asked if he was interested in getting a band together and suggested that, devoid of drums, Andrew should be the singer. The outfit eventually emerged in the mid seventies as The Stickers. "It was a sort of pub rock band, similar to what Graham Parker and Elvis Costello were doing at that point. It was quite good but too diverse: we had a couple of reggae numbers, a couple of country and western and a couple of blues. It just wasn't consistent enough and after two or three years broke up acrimoniously."

Soon afterwards, Ranken formed The Operation, recruiting keyboards and bassist via his special friend Deborah's two brothers, Joe and Simon. "I also managed to involve this guy called Phil Langran, who played guitar and was very good at getting people together. He just started bringing more and more people along, then all their friends kept turning up – every week there was someone new. But it was good fun, and it sounded all right 'cos everyone could play pretty well."

The Operation spawned into an enormous line-up, up to 13, usually including Paul Hookham (who later joined The Woodentops and The Redskins). The band earned a phenomenal reputation for busking: their cajun r 'n' b regularly brought in £100 from the Covent Garden voyeurs, and they also favoured a spot just beneath Waterloo Bridge.

"There was a bar with tables and chairs just outside the National Film Theatre, and we'd start up just as the audience were leaving, which was great during the summer evenings. The Operation

were the kind of band who'd play anywhere; we did all sorts of weird places like kids' adventure playgrounds."

Throughout the seventies Andrew had a series of temporary jobs, but in 1981 he decided to return to college and take Communication Studies and Sociology at Goldsmiths. Meanwhile, The Operation continued to play around London; they attracted a strong following but took themselves less than seriously.

Consequently, it wasn't too difficult for Finer and MacGowan to persuade Ranken to have a second shot at manning the Pogue sticks.

"Jem and Shane had come up with this idea of how they wanted the drums to sound," says Andrew. "It was completely different to the usual way of playing: I was doing with my right hand what you'd normally do with your foot on the bass drum. It was like only having half as much, and

trying to get a decent sound with very little. So it was quite a challenge."

From the very first practice it was obvious that Andrew was exactly what Pogue Mahone needed. And, although he was reluctant to make a full-time commitment, Ranken was equally impressed by the band. "I used to go to a lot of Irish pubs in London so I loved the music," he says. "I'd been to a few English folk clubs and they really pissed me off 'cos their whole approach was so reverent, but The Pogues weren't doing it like that at all. It was really exciting, back to the basic thing, and the melodies were great."

Andrew gave his quare kit its first airing at Islington's Hope And Anchor, at the beginning of March 1983. Shortly afterwards, Country Jem went from a jack to a king by marrying Marcia, his close companion for the past three years. Their wedding party was a night of madness

and mayhem in Smithy's Wine Bar, on the King's Cross Road, culminating in a memorably schlewtered set from the band.

'A sinking ship in a sea of sharks/Is no safe place to be/A passing doubt/When passing out/Is not much for company.' (Ranken).

Pogue Mahone spent the next six months stamping their sound on North London. They now attracted a regular crowd, and before long were filling the pubs – although there were still some dodgy nights like the time they played to five people at The Pindar of Wakefield. Or the night they faced a crowd of 16 in The Hope And Anchor and the promoter told them, as politely as he could, "I don't think you're the kind of band that's suited to playing here."

Their fierce thirst rapidly evolved into legend, and their gigs were characterized by drink, disorder and drink. "We were blind drunk whenever we did it," admits Shane. "We were blind drunk because people kept buying us drinks! But there was an energy there, an energy that wasn't going on at the time. There wasn't anybody actually getting up in places like The Hope And Anchor, The Bull And Gate or the Pindar and playing dance music with tunes. And we just thought, fuck it, what we're doing is good however badly we're doing it, it's good 'cos it's based on good music. It's emotional. It's what songs are about."

With The Pogues, nothing was sacred. Their repertoire readily embraced everything from 'Poor Paddy' and 'Me And Bobby McGee' to The Nips' 'King Of The Bop' and the Velvets' 'All Tomorrows Parties'. But arguments as to which song they should sing next were invariable. These usually led to a huddled discussion-cum-row, stage centre, and occasionally degenerated into a drunken brawl, more often than not between Shane and the formidable Cait (who quickly won the title of 'Rocky').

Their equipment remained as basic as their approach; the only signs of technology were a small bass amp and Spider's beer tray. The Pogues used instruments traditionally associated with folk, yet played them with all the verve and passion of punk.

"The whole thing had a very unique sound," says Jem, "'cos it was learnt in a completely accidental way. We were just a bunch of *useless* musicians trying to play Irish folk music. And, obviously, it turned out completely different."

In mid-summer, The Pogues committed their improved Ranken formula to tape. They turned to their Pindar friends, Justin and Vicki, and – having hired an eight-track – transformed the Wards' flat into a recording studio. The result was a demo of five songs, the most outstanding of which was 'Streams Of Whiskey'.

By July, Pogue Mahone had captured the attention of the press, as well as the imagination of a growing public. And among the most ardent of their admirers was Philip Chevron. "It was irrelevant how well or how badly they played Irish music," he says. "It really didn't matter. They just had a magic that other groups simply didn't have."

James – whose ability to tune all the instruments had earned him the nickname 'Maestro' – had originally stressed that if Pogue Mahone interfered with his writing then he would have to leave. But by this time his faith in the band had increased, and he downed his pen and threw his creativity into music.

Meanwhile, Spider had come a long way from 'Silent Night' and piped a tune of his own. It was a rousing instrumental, which he made up one afternoon while watching Play School, and which was christened in true Stacy style, 'Repeal Of The Licensing Laws'.

That August, Caitlin launched her singing career. Down at The Pindar Of Wakefield, where a group called The Boothill Foot-tappers were playing, she bumped into Darryl Hunt, whom she had first encountered some months before – when she was sprawled across a pub floor after a fight with Shane – but who was now a frequent face among The Pogues, and sometimes drove their gear to gigs.

Darryl and his erstwhile friend and musical partner, Dave Scott, were discussing their plans for a new band at the bar. They were, they told Cait, fed up with writing their own material and were going to play their favourite jazz numbers instead. They had come to the Pindar to find a singer, and were thinking of asking the Boothill's Wendy May. Cait laughed with searing derision and immediately said, "I'll do it."

Prior to this, O'Riordan had confined her singing to the bathroom. "I'd sung backing vocals of a sort, on stage, with The Pogues," she admits, "but if you ever heard the tapes you'd know why I never got invited to the front."

She auditioned with a few bars of 'And Don't It Make My Brown Eyes Blue' and was told, "You can't sing, but we can't play." Thus began Pride Of The Cross.

Pogue Mahone rarely played more than once a week, so Pride Of The Cross were able to make monthly appearances at the Pindar. Their set was famous for its covers: Dionne Warwick, Peggy Lee and, most notably, Abba's 'The Day Before You Came'. It was the Radio 2 fodder that Cait knew (and loved) by heart.

In September, Andrew returned to Goldsmiths for his final year of Communication Studies. For the past six months, he had combined his college work with both Pogue Mahone and The Operation and frequently had to cancel Pogue gigs. Much to their irritation the others would have to find a last-minute replacement in The Sting-ray's drummer Alec.

But as the summer nights closed into autumn, and The Operation began to dwindle, Ranken finally conceded that his busking days were over and put his heart into The Pogues. He marked the occasion by nicknaming himself after one of their songs, 'The Clobberer'.

By the time they celebrated their first birthday The Pogues had acquired a significant following. Their manic mix of furious punk, Irish folk and rampant rockabilly was certainly like no other. The psychotic dementia of Spider, blitzing his brains out with a beer-tray, was a highlight of their show and yet, in complete contrast, when Shane slowed into 'And The Band Played Waltzing Matilda', the sheer soul could tear the place apart.

"It was obvious right from the start that, in a way, we were actually serious," says Andrew, "and

Pride Of The Cross

that we were trying to do something that hadn't been done before. We had no idea whether it was going to work or not, but we thought it was worth a try and we also thought it was good for a laugh, and we were all into having a laugh. And one of the most important things for me was that it ought to be really good fun to do gigs, or go to a gig and see the sort of band that we were trying to be. It's a terrible cliché but we did genuinely want to have a good time doing what we were doing, and we wanted lots of people to come and see us and have a good time as well."

At this point, various record companies got wise and BMW-driving A&R men were suddenly out in force. Among the bands with whom Pogue Mahone sometimes shared a bill, were a rockabilly

31

quartet called The Shillelagh Sisters. In November, the Shillelaghs were snapped up by CBS. But The Pogues' uninhibited mania was too much to stomach. The A&Rs scurried away. Perplexed.

Meanwhile, the band were fast becoming the pride of North London, with Ted Carroll's Rock On record store in Camden Town a main bastion of Pogue support. Among the Rock On fraternity/ London Murphia was Frank Murray, a man with a 15-year pedigree in the rock business, and it was on Carroll's suggestion that Murray – and his friend Dave Jordan – went to see Pogue Mahone at the Hope And Anchor.

What they witnessed was an anarchic version of The Dubliners and – if legend is to be believed – Murray stood there open mouthed. "There came a point," says Frank, "when people thought that they'd discovered folk in inverted commas, and a snobbery came into the music so that people were going into Cecil Sharp House and spending days on end trying to find obscure ballads so they could say, 'This is a song I learnt from Sitting Bull', or whatever. So bands like The Dubliners and The Clancy Brothers, who played in the old singalong tradition became unfashionable, and one had to be like Planxty or The Bothy Band who were, I suppose, more scholarly.

"And I wasn't sure what hit me first about The Pogues, but they just got better and better. They did 'Dirty Old Town' and 'Peggy Gordon' and then Cait came out for the encore and sang 'And Don't It Make My Brown Eyes Blue'. Yet at the same time, the whole stage was so dishevelled that they were like a total mess: there were people bumping into each other all over the place. It was kind of like slapstick, except it wasn't feigned and there was nothing pretentious. They were just having a great time."

But although Murray was struck by the spirit of The Pogues, he realized that their shambolic ways would make for a manager's nightmare. He was, after all, used to the likes of Thin Lizzy, Elton John, The Commodores and Blue Oyster Cult,

and he was later reputed to have commented that The Pogues 'were too undisciplined for his consideration.

The Pogue experience, however, continued to spread and, in December, *Music Week* magazine ran a poll among disc-jockeys, journalists and record company employees, to find out which artists were most likely (and deserving) to succeed in 1984. The vote went to Pogue Mahone.

New Year came though with still no record deal in sight. "The record companies had been sniffing around for months," says Shane, "and they came along, and there were packed audiences going crazy, but they just couldn't understand it. They came and they saw us blasting it out, and people going nuts, but they couldn't understand why they were going nuts so they couldn't see how they could market us, so they fucked off again."

The band decided to forget about recording contracts and make a cut-price video instead. It was to be a promotional reel for their demo of 'Streams Of Whiskey' (which they had recorded at Justin and Vicki Wards', the previous summer), and even though it wasn't of a good enough quality to be released as a single, everyone agreed that a video would be a good crack. The technology was supplied by Richard Elgard – also known as Video Rick – who was keen to capture The Pogues on film, and could shoot it for around £60, considerably less than one per cent of the average video budget.

The initial location was Hillview tenements, around their King's Cross home, and the opening sequence saw the band emerging from corporation dustbins. It continued with some appalling breakdancing from James; Spider battering his head against a brick wall and a spritely stepdance from Cait. It also featured Shane and Jem, stripped to their underpants, sitting in deckchairs on the drained bed of the Camden Canal.

"It was basically pisstakes of lots of other videos," says Jem. "The canal scene is a pisstake of Wham! in Club Tropicana, where they sit by the

pool drinking champagne. It was the coldest day of the year, and Shane and I sat on the canal bed – with no clothes on – surrounded by broken bottles, rusty prams and sludge and drank cider from champagne glasses.''

The video came to a grand finale when The Pogues hired the backroom of The Pindar Of Wakefield and – after packing the place with friends – tipped over a huge table of drinks, to send streams of beer and whiskey flying.

Simultaneously, Stan Brennan offered to put up the money for a Pogue Mahone single. It was subsequently agreed that Brennan – the man behind The Nips' recordings – would issue the single as a one-off on Rocks Off, until he could find a licensing deal.

'Dark Streets Of London' was consequently recorded at Elephant Studios in late January, 1984. Produced by Brennan, it summed up the inimit-

able rough flavour of Pogue Mahone, with cheering chorus of tin whistle, banjo and accordion, and also hinted that MacGowan might be a promising songwriter. 'Dark Streets' was coupled with Eric Bogle's 'And The Band Played Waltzing Matilda' but on record it failed to capture the magic of live performance.

Ironically, at the same time that Pogue Mahone committed themselves to vinyl, their spiritual mentor died. Luke Kelly was the sublime lead singer of The Dubliners, and it was from them – and Luke in particular – that The Pogues derived their greatest inspiration.

In February, Pogue Mahone were invited to record a Radio 1 session for John Peel. They chose four tracks: 'Streams Of Whiskey', Brendan Behan's 'The Auld Triangle', 'Greenland Whale Fisheries' – a traditional song made famous by The Dubliners – and a crazed country blues number which MacGowan had titled 'Boys From The County Hell'.

But The Pogues were almost ejected from the studio before they got started. Cait turned up completely blotto, totally oblivious to BBC decorum. The engineers did their best to ignore her, and recording eventually commenced. But, 'Boys From The County Hell' contained one too many cusses even for the Peel show, and only three tracks were broadcast.

At this stage, The Pogues were managing themselves, with responsibilities shared between Finer and MacGowan. Shane was the creative end of the partnership, and Jem the business side – which seemed to encompass everything.

"It used to be my dream," says Finer, "to have someone working for us who would move gear. At the time we only had about seven items, but I always had to arrange who drove these items around, and I always had to find someone to help me and basically it was always me and James."

In March, Pogue Mahone were offered their first date outside London when Wolverhampton Student Union asked them to play the polytechnic

on Saint Patrick's Night. The fee was insufficient to cover van and petrol costs but rather than turn the gig down, Jem had the speculative notion of hiring a coach and recruiting a crowd to go along with them. The other Pogues thought it was worth a try and started flogging tickets.

Meanwhile, The Clash were set for a comeback with a hat-trick of dates at Brixton Academy between March 8-10. Shane had known Joe Strummer for years, and asked him for a support slot. Strummer agreed, and Pogue Mahone subsequently played to a packed Academy.

"The crowd came in as soon as the doors opened," says Spider, "so we essentially played to a full house, and that was a really good experience." The Pogues won many new fans that night, including The Clash.

The following week, 2000 white label copies of 'Dark Streets Of London' were issued. The Pogues promoted it to wild advantage, with a steamy Saint Patrick's party at Camden Irish Centre.

The next day, March 17, was the real thing. With shamrocks to the fore, and The Bothy Band in the tape-deck, the Pogue army headed for Wolverhampton. "The trip was astonishingly successful, financially," says Jem. "We filled the coach up with Pogue Mahone fans, and it all went off very well except that these people were completely mad. They all came on with at least 12 packs of beer, and it was obvious that something horrendous was going to happen."

The tickets were sold on the basis that they would cover entrance to the gig as well as the

return journey. But when the coach arrived at the polytechnic, the Student Union was apparently unaware of the pilgrimage, and 40 ticketless, irate and totally flutered Pogue fans took to the streets of Wolverhampton instead.

After the gig, The Pogues – who were not entirely sober themselves – reloaded their stinking cargo and hoped for the best. But before they hit the M1, disaster struck. Says Jem, "The tank in the toilet burst, so it took about seven hours to get home 'cos we had to keep stopping for people to get off. And when we picked our gear out from underneath, it was all just soaked in piss."

Three days later, and Pogue Mahone were heading out of London again. This time, they were special guests at the Jericho Folk Club in Oxford. "That was a really strange gig," remembers Spider. "It was a really folky audience who were so polite that they even clapped the sound check! But they treated us really well: the prices at the bar were slashed to a third of their normal price, and that went on for as long as we wanted with no hassles at all."

That weekend, however, Shane's Saturday night out in Camden Town came to an abrupt end when he was severely beaten, for no apparent reason, in the Electric Ballroom toilets.

The following evening, MacGowan arrived at the 100 Club, half-dazed and with the left hand side of his face swollen to the size of a melon. He managed to stumble on stage, and The Pogues began with 'Greenland Whale Fisheries'. But after a few slurred verses Stan Brennan called the concussed singer to one side, and Spider took over on vocals. Meanwhile, Stephan Cush – an irrepressible busker and occasional Pogue roadie – grabbed Shane's guitar and strummed his way through their shortened set.

It was while Shane was putting his face back together that Hokum Hillbilly hit its height. The music press suddenly picked up on the country based sounds of the Boothill Foot-tappers, Helen And The Horns, Hackney Five-O, and a host of other bands Born Again In Wild West London, and soon everyone had a checked shirt, a hay bale haircut and a banjo. The Pogues were inevitably roped in.

Still, the only bad publicity is no publicity, as Shane openly admitted: "I'm quite prepared to ride any bandwagon that is going to get us somewhere." And so, on Easter Monday, while Glen Campbell, The Osmond Brothers and Roly Daniels were playing the hallowed annual country music festival at Wembley, Pogue Mahone joined the Boothill Foot-tappers, Hackney Five-O, the Blubbery Hellbellies and the Skiff Skats in an Alternative Country Festival at the Electric Ballroom.

Among the audience was a handful of friends, including both Cush and Shanne (who had formed The Nipple Erectors and subsequent Nips with Shane). Midway through the proceedings, they borrowed The Pogues' gear, their drummer and accordion player, and took to the stage with a set of covers: 'A Boy Named Sue', 'Where Have All The Flowers Gone?' and anything else they could think of. The Men They Couldn't Hang had played their first gig.

Simultaneously, London Weekend Television zoomed in on countrypunkabilly via its *South Of Watford Show*. The programme featured Pogue Mahone, The Shillelagh Sisters, The Boothill Foot-tappers and The Skiff Skats, with the main focus falling on the CBS signed Shillelaghs.

After several rounds of live Pogue Mahone footage, Shane articulated the main difference between The Pogues and traditional Irish bar bands. "The stuff we play is more fucked up – 'cos you are more fucked up if you live in London than if you live in a nice little town in Tipperary."

The LWT censors were less than impressed, and presenter Ben Elton concluded, "I think it will be a while before Pogue Mahone – Gaelic for kiss my arse, by the way – are on *Top Of The Pops*. Some of the other bands may stand a better chance of breaking through to a wider audience. But in the long run, it's likely that countrybilly will stay where it's at its best – in the boozy, sweaty, raw atmosphere of live performance."

The record companies were equally astute. Although John Peel, David Jensen and even Mike Read were championing 'Dark Streets Of London', Stan Brennan was still slogging from one major to the next.

But by the end of the month Pogue Mahone had become a nationwide name. An eagle-eared producer on BBC Radio Scotland, listening to the Mike Read show, was affronted by the tasteless term 'pogue mahone'. As a member of the Gaelic speaking community, he was outraged to hear the words 'kiss my arse' at three o'clock in the afternoon, and he figured that thousands (if not millions) of Gaelic speaking listeners would be equally offended. After a quick call to head office The Pogues were banned from further airplay on Radio Scotland.

Down at Radio 1, they were less anxious to fan the flames of a potential controversy. They had, after all, just recovered from the Frankie Goes To Hollywood fiasco, which hurtled 'Relax' into the list of all time best selling hits. And so, rather than ban the record, the BBC decided to freeze it: the DJs wouldn't play 'Dark Streets' because they couldn't say the name of the group – all that is – apart from John Peel who, after 10 o'clock at night, could say 'kiss my arse' in any language he chose as many times as he liked.

In May, having been turned down by most of the major labels, Stan Brennan took 'Dark Streets Of London' to Stiff. The company showed genuine enthusiasm and immediately agreed to re-release the single. They did stipulate one condition though: the band would have to abbreviate their name to The Pogues, since there was little point in issuing a record that wouldn't get played.

"That wasn't a problem," says Jem, "people called us The Pogues anyway, because Pogue Mahone is a bit of a mouthful. Besides, the name was never an attempt to be controversial, it was just a joke. At the time, no one liked it much; it was just a name."

The Pogues subsequently signed a one-off single deal with Stiff, with an option on an LP and another single. But it was no secret that the record company wanted them to curtail their wayward ways in order to make business dealings easier, and the band were soon said to be drinking milk and to have taken up jogging. Publicity shots depicting a very sombre and conspicuously bottleless bunch did little to dispel the rumours.

"When we first signed to Stiff," says Shane, "we had to pretend we'd stopped drinking. So in the photo sessions, we had to hide our drinks. And in the pictures we look really miserable and uncomfortable because we're sitting on our beer-cans."

But it would take a greater force than Stiff to stifle Pogue Mahone, and they were soon sharing a bill with their long-time friends and reprobate label mates King Kurt on a short tour of London.

On June 22, The Pogues played alongside a doom and gloom merchant from Factory Records in central London's Diorama. The depression was exacerbated by the fact that alcohol was banned from the venue. Nevertheless, among the crowd was Elvis Costello, lately pointed in The Pogues' direction by an ever-enthusing Philip Chevron. Suitably impressed, Costello invited the band to accompany him on his autumn tour.

By now, Cait was attracting attention for her monthly appearances in Pride Of The Cross. Dietrich-style, O'Riordan would don dark glasses and beret and – beneath the glare of a stark spotlight – pump out 'Fever', 'Is That All There Is?' and 'The Day Before You Came', then waver through the melancholy moments of 'Black Coffee' and 'I Sold My Heart To The Junkman'.

Among the most memorable of Pride Of The Cross performances was a closing down show at The Hope And Anchor. The bar was lit by candlelight, and warmed by the power of Cait's voice. "She had a natural charm on stage," says POTC bassist Darryl. "She could get up and make a song that everyone had heard a million times before sound like it had been written for her. It didn't matter whether she hit the right notes or whatever, she just had it. A true chanteuse."

In July, however, Pogue commitments increased. They were now playing twice a week – taking them from Hammersmith to Harrow and from Carlton Community Centre to Harlesden's Mean Fiddler – and, at the same time, Stiff asked them to record an LP.

Consequently, Cait had to buckle down to her bass, and there was no time for Pride Of The Cross. But before drawing a final curtain they recorded a one-off single at Elephant Studios. 'Tommy's Blue Valentine' is a song which Phil Gaston wrote for Cait as a tribute to her hero, Tom Waits. The music was penned by Darryl Hunt and Dave Scott, and the record also features the trombone playing of Paul Taylor. It was backed with a cover of Peggy Lee's 'Black Coffee', and both tracks were produced by Phil Gaston.

Meanwhile, The Pogues had begun work on 'Red Roses For Me', a blend of MacGowan originals and traditional rearrangements. It was produced by Stan Brennan, and recorded at Elephant Studios throughout August.

At the same time, they continued to play around the capital. As a live act, The Pogues might have wiped out the whole of London's North, North-West and even West One, but their performances were still as shambolic as they were exciting, their arguments as frequent as they were pathetic.

They were banned from Wardour Street's Wag Club – after an on-stage fight between Rocky O'Riordan and Mouth MacGowan developed into unarmed combat in the dressing room, and, on August 8, MacGowan and Finer almost came to serious blows at the Sir George Robey, in Finsbury Park.

"Shane used to do really irritating things," says Jem. "We'd learn a new song and then have an argument to get it put in the set, and we'd just be about to do it when Shane'd shake his head and say, 'Nah, nah, nah', and we'd all stand around for five minutes discussing what we were going to do next."

On this particular night, Jem was actually playing the intro to 'And The Band Played Waltzing Matilda' when Shane suddenly announced that he was going to sing a Phil Gaston song called 'Navigator' instead. A furious row followed, which was on the verge of becoming physical when Cait butted in. Finer immediately turned from MacGowan to her: there was a pint glass at his foot and he took a well aimed kick. The glass shot into the air, flew across the stage and finally splattered precariously close to O'Riordan's head.

Says James: "The thing I really like about this band is that we're always arguing but no one gets upset for long. In the other groups I was in, if you disagreed with someone then they'd go off in a huff. But with The Pogues, tempers explode and it just clears the air."

By the end of August, The Pogues were preparing for their October-long tour with Elvis Costello And The Attractions. Rehearsals took place, as ever, in the tiny back room of a tenement flat. Simultaneously, however, they received their first taste of luxury: Stiff splashed out on six pale blue duster coats, tailored to the Wild And Willing tune of £100 each. Similar garb had been worn by the notorious James Gang in the Walter Hill Western

Darryl Hunt

Long Riders, and Shane had decided this was perfect stage gear for The Pogues.

But when they got round to modelling the coats, in the 'Red Roses For Me' photo-session, MacGowan was looking less than his film star best. He had been involved in a late night collision with three flights of stairs, suffered a broken ankle and now carried a stick.

And there were further afflictions: by the time they realized that the front cover photos would have to be re-done, Andrew had disappeared on holiday. A small Ranken mugshot was subsequently slapped beneath the rest of the band.

It was in similar haphazard fashion that they recorded a video for 'Waxies Dargle'. Shot in Camden's Irish Centre, it featured Darryl Hunt on drums and – since Jem was also on holiday – a behatted imposter on banjo. All the same, the result was gloriously hellbent. The focus fell on the crazed Caitlin and Spider's terminal masochism: he bashed his forehead with a beer tray four times in each verse, 32 times per song and, after nine takes, had inflicted a total of 288 blows on the Stacy bonce.

A couple of weeks later it was time for the Elvis Costello tour, which opened in Northern Ireland, but before heading out, The Pogues invited Darryl Hunt to take on the all-encompassing role of van driver cum roadie.

Born the son of a fisherman, in Hampshire, Darryl Hunt started playing guitar when he was 10-years-old.

"My brother Ian was in a rock 'n' roll group in Bournemouth and he was really good at playing guitar; he knew all the licks. I never learnt to play from a classical point of view, I just knew the riffs of the latest hits. So the first thing I played was soul: Booker T And The MGs, Tamla and stuff."

When Darryl was in his teens, the Hunts moved to Devon where his interest in music was overshadowed by art and, after doing a two-year foundation course at a local college, he went to Nottingham to study Fine Art, where he started playing in a group called Plummet Airline. In 1976, the band got their hair cut and abandoned the college circuit for the pubs of London.

One night, Stiff boss Dave Robinson saw them playing at The Hope And Anchor and invited them to record 'Silver Shirt' as one of the first singles on his newly established label. "Stiff had just started, so we used to sit in the office putting singles in their sleeves. That's how we met up with The Damned and we often played with them."

After Plummet Airline broke up at the beginning of 1978, Darryl joined a Nottingham power pop group known as The Favourites, then came to London again where, ensconced in a King's Cross squat, he formed a doo wop punk band called The Lemons, and did a stint of tour managing with the Mo-dettes.

During the course of The Lemons, Darryl got together with his art college friend, Dave Scott (who had played in both Spizz Energi and Athletico Spizz '80) and formed a part-time group which they christened Baby Lotion.

"But then," says Darryl, "we got fed up with the whole capitalist, careerist business and we just wanted to play our favourite tunes; murdering them but having a good time."

It was then, in the summer of 1983, that they went to The Pindar Of Wakefield, chanced across Cait O'Riordan and formed Pride Of The Cross. "The band was never intended to be serious, but people really liked it and it was great fun to do."

After a year of monthly gigs, the band recorded 'Tommy's Blue Valentine' as a single. "By that time The Pogues were getting really busy so we decided to knock Pride Of The Cross on the head,

41

which was a disappointment for me and Dave 'cos we'd rated Cait very highly."

And so, his musical outlets temporarily thwarted, Darryl agreed to work with The Pogues. He filled a C90 with Seamus Ennis, The Bothy Band, Dubliners, Clancy Brothers and Jolly Beggarmen and, on September 26, steered their hired Transit towards the Holyhead ferry.

Having arrived in Dun Laoghaire, The Pogues spent a night in Dublin before driving to Belfast for their opening show at Ulster Hall. Since this was to be their first Irish date, there was a feeling of apprehension, not at the magnitude of the venue but at the thought of taking coal to Cork.

"There's no living folk tradition in England," said Shane, "and that's the whole point about why we're doing what we do. But in Ireland there are lots of bands doing a similar thing, so I don't actually see that there's any point in us playing."

But The Pogues needn't have worried, Belfast took their untamed set straight to its heart. "We blew Costello off stage," asserts Spider. "Well, we didn't exactly blow him off stage, but the Belfast audience is really good, very appreciative – and it was brilliant. I don't think we were ever actually scared of playing in front of an audience in a big hall, but when you're used to playing in little clubs and pubs, the first time that you go out on a huge stage it feels really weird."

What the band didn't realize, though, was that they were expected to pay for both the lighting and the PA. "The gig money was threatened with extinction on the very first gig," says James. "We were getting about £100, but they said that we would have to pay £60 to the lighting and sound men. That would have meant losing two-thirds of our income, so somebody – Elvis, I think – haggled on our behalf and we ended up with just a third of it going."

The following day, they travelled south westward to Galway, eventually arriving at the Leisureland ballroom two hours behind the scheduled time, only to find that their gear was still at the Ulster Hall. "For some reason, best known to themselves," recounts Spider, "Costello's road crew managed to mistake a case full of BBC Radio oboes for our flight case. So when we arrived in Galway, a little bit late, they presented us with a load of oboes! We said, 'Well that's not really much help' and the guy who was handling the gear turned round and said, 'If you hadn't been late your gear would have been here' – I think he was speaking in Philadelphia time! But we ended up having to play on electric instruments."

While their electric show went down well enough, Galway itself was not without further incident. The city was the scene of a late summer festival and so, before leaving, The Pogues went in search of some Connaught action.

Darryl parked the van outside a late night bar, and James and Cait volunteered to check out the scene. But they hadn't even reached the entrance before Cait's spiky coiffure was attracting uncomplimentary attention. "Will you look at herself," leered one less than sober youth, "with her hair shticking up like she do be frightened." The insults continued to fly but O'Riordan – to the amazement of her colleagues – refused to take the bait and calmly returned to the van. After several minutes, the loudest of the locals poked his head through the door to view the spectacle at closer range.

Without saying a word, Cait leapt to her feet, reached for the handle and ZAP! her tormentor's nose was splattered by the transit door. There was no time for mercy as the Irishman screamed, the blood flowed and The Pogues got the hell out of town.

They arrived at Dublin's National Stadium feeling all the worse for their coast to coast trek. "We were completely useless," admits Spider, "but the crowd were pretty tolerant. They just thought, they'll be off stage soon, they're only a support band. But then Elvis proceeded to fuck up too: five minutes into the set he decided he'd lost his voice, disappeared for 20 minutes and then came back on again. So we blew him off stage there as well."

But after the show, Stacy descended into the drunken doldrums: stumbling and falling until he eventually collapsed on the South Circular Road. "I just lay in the street thinking, 'Shit, I've ripped my suit. My new suit. Bollocks! I'm just gonna stay here until a car runs over my head then I won't be pissed off any more 'cos I'll be dead.' But I got picked up and put in the van, and Andrew bathed my wound in Listerine."

The Pogues retired to the scene of Joyce's *Ulysses* The Ormond Hotel, where Julie Pritchard – a close friend of Darryl's who was on tour to sell T-shirts – waged war against an unsuspecting window.

Reluctant to spend a cold, rainy night sleeping in the van, Julie settled into the hotel lobby instead. But before long, she was turfed out by an inhospitable porter. Seconds later came the vengeful crash of breaking glass: a brick through the window, a £45 stitch in Ormond expenses and another black hole in The Pogues' reputation.

Returning to London, the band played the first of five Monday night shows at the Hammersmith Palais and, four days later, 'Waxies Dargle' was transmitted around the country via *The Tube*. Such was the impact of Spider and his beer tray, that the video was a candidate for the *Europe A Go-Go* music extravaganza. It was a neat coincidence that the band had chosen the same week to release their début LP.

A rough and ready mixture of the traditional and their own, 'Red Roses For Me' was an accurate assessment of the story so far. Opening with the thundering nihilism of 'Transmetropolitan', through 'The Battle Of Brisbane' and 'Waxies Dargle' to a passionate, if imperfect, rendition of Brendan Behan's 'The Auld Triangle'. The rest of side one ably illustrated the force of MacGowan's pen with 'Boys From The County Hell', 'Dark Streets Of London' and the bitter 'Sea Shanty', the tale of a washed up sailor.

The other side began with two of their most well-worn favourites 'Streams Of Whiskey' and 'Poor Paddy', followed by 'Dingle Regatta' and a vigorous charge through 'Greenland Whale Fisheries'. 'Down In The Ground Where The Dead Men Go' brought a Pogue eye view of the Irish famine graves, featuring the unintelligible vocals, piercing shrieks and sonorous screams of Shane and Spider. But the record closed with 'Kitty', a poignant tale of love, internment and separation. It was a ballad which was performed live with only varying degrees of success, but whose genuine heartbreak was perfectly translated on to vinyl.

"'Kitty' is my favourite track on the album," says Shane. "It's a song that I learnt from my mother and I've only ever met one person, who wasn't out of my family or from round our particular little area in Tipperary, who knows it."

Although 'Red Roses' managed to capture The Pogues in all their gut-grabbing glory, the overall sound left much to be desired. Nevertheless its strength and originality value made it flavour of the week with the music press.

The inclusion of Behan's 'The Auld Triangle', supplemented by the anti-establishment ethos of their own 'Transmetropolitan' and 'Boys From The County Hell', sparked queries as to whether or not they held Republican sympathies. Non-

committally, MacGowan replied that their political persuasions had nothing to do with what they were playing as a band. "What we're saying is fuck everything," he says. "Which is not the same as saying fuck so and so." With 'Red Roses For Me' as a sure-fire flogger, The Pogues took the music they loved to the nation at large. It was almost a crusade.

"The thing about Pogue music," says Cait, "is that people will listen to it more than they would to TR Dallas or Mary O'Hara. They'd just have it in their heads that Irish music is stuff like 'The Old Bell On The High Road' – but it's not! There's still 'Waxies Dargle', 'Seven Drunken Nights', the real rollickin' stuff that you don't get to hear 'cos it's not tidied up enough for the radio."

With a single flight-case to their name, the band were spared from the burden of heavy equipment. As they travelled from one city hall to another, the organisers would invariably ask, "Where's your truck?". "Where's the bar? Where's the stage? Give us the money!" came the Pogue reply. Their van was filled, instead, with the sound of The Dubliners and Clancy Brothers, and the constant rattle of empty cans and bottles.

Descending on Portsmouth, on October 7, all the better for a long Sunday session, Cait launched a one-woman riot. It began with a single bottle, which she casually lobbed from a back stage window, and developed into a non-stop shower.

What O'Riordan failed to take into account, though, was that Costello's road crew were unloading their lorries directly beneath. Says Andrew: "They all chased after her, so she smashed a bottle and came running upstairs with another in her hand. I wrestled with her and – just as they burst into the dressing room – managed to disarm her and hide the missile behind my back."

Costello's men failed to get the joke, and it took powerful persuasion from Elvis himself to stop The Pogues being kicked off the tour. For Cait, the incident was merely one in a series of corned capers and is only vaguely recollected at all. "I just

drunk steadily for about two years," she says. "I never even thought about not drinking, so all I remember is getting horribly drunk."

On the road, under the stars and perpetually at the bottle, The Pogues headed west. En route to St Austell's Coliseum, they came upon a Newton Abbot cider bar where they knocked back as much scrumpy as their stomachs could stand. Jem, James and Andrew eventually staggered out with a stolen trayfull, knocked back the contents and presented Spider with a brand new instrument.

A couple of nights later they hit the unlikely oasis of Bristol. Jem decided to act out a Leone scenario and – after cutting two holes in the lining of his duster coat – filled both pockets with sand, pulled down his straw hat and staggered on stage.

"I looked like I'd just come in from the desert," he says, "leaving a trail of sand everywhere I walked."

Unfortunately, some of the sand found its way into Steve Nieve's keyboards, and the episode did nothing to further endear The Pogues to The Attractions.

The following day it was back to Hammersmith Palais, where The Pogues re-decorated their dressing room walls, burnt a hole in the carpet and let off a few explosives. The reprobates were consequently denied a soundcheck and literally blown off stage by that night's other support, The Men They Couldn't Hang.

During the evening, various Pogues wandered into the pub next door, and Jem got talking to Frank Murray who was down at the Palais to watch The Men They Couldn't Hang. Murray had an extensive knowledge of the music business, and he and Finer had a lengthy conversation.

The Pogues spent the next few days in the Midlands. After their gig at Loughborough University – where their childish antics had earned them another yellow card from Costello's tour manager – they ended up having a drunken argument in the van.

After a few minutes, Jem was so aggravated by

Shane and Spider that he ordered Darryl to stop the van and set off on the 15-mile walk to Nottingham. Most of The Pogues shrugged with unconcern, but it wasn't long before Spider bleated, "Stop! I'm walking too."

"I was walking along the road for ages," remembers Stacy. "First of all I was thinking, 'If the van comes back I'm going to pretend I haven't seen it.' But it never came and after a while I started getting a bit worried that I might actually have to walk to Nottingham. Then I saw the van coming and, for some reason, I got nervous and stepped off the grass verge and moved further into the countryside. But unfortunately I got in the way of a ditch, into which I fell, and even more unfortunately it was full of stinging nettles."

By this time, Jem had caught up with the commotion. "I had sat on a grass verge for about 10 minutes, drank a beer, then thought I'd better set off and hitch a lift. I was quite content, walking along, but I went round the corner and there was the bloody van with the lights on, and everyone shouting for Spider."

While Jem climbed back aboard, Shane and Cait attempted to rescue the stinging Stacy. "They grabbed hold of my hands to pull me out, and I dragged them in on top of me," he laughs. "But then we all jumped back in the van, and lived happily ever after."

By this time, The Pogues had backed 'Boys From The County Hell' with Stacy's 'Repeal Of The Licensing Laws' and, on October 22, it was released as their second single. This time round, MacGowan's lyrics were toned down for daytime consumption and the song was notable for its bottleneck guitar and genius refrain, 'Lend me £10 and I'll buy you a drink.'

The following day they arrived in Leeds, and while Costello checked into the city square's classy Dragonara Hotel The Pogues found themselves in a gay temperance hotel.

"It was the most disgusting place you can imagine," says Jem. "The wallpaper was mushy pea coloured; everything clashed and it was all dank and cold and depressing. And in the morning, there were all these really bad drawings of muscle-bound pretty young men with leather jockstraps on lining the walls of the breakfast room, and there was this extremely homosexual young lad trying to be sophisticated and suave but serving up greasy platefuls of sausage, bacon and eggs with a broad Yorkshire accent."

The experience had to be worth something, and the band decided on a half-hearted stab at self-publicity. They made out they'd smuggled bottles into their rooms for a post-midnight party, and when the booze-up was discovered they were booted out and ordered never to return. "We weren't really banned," admits Finer. "For a laugh, we just phoned up the ever-gullible press office at Stiff and said that we'd been banned from every temperance society hotel in the country, and it got printed – which isn't surprising, 'cos it's the sort of rubbish they like to put in the papers."

The Pogues somehow managed to make it to the end of the tour, winding up a week later in Norwich with a screaming profile and 'Red Roses For Me' in increasing demand.

"That was a great tour," says James. "It really was. Some of the things that happened . . . But one of my clearest memories is of Jem sitting in the back of the van: we had 'the office' – which was a shortbread tin that my mum had once given to me with some sandwiches in – and it had a cheque book in it, a notebook, a pen and the petty cash. And nearly every day, Jem would say, 'Can I have the office, please?' and he'd work out how much money we were losing. Then he'd sit in the back of the van, with his feet over the seat in front, tapping his teeth with a pen, just looking through the window."

Back in London it was clear that a biscuit tin would no longer suffice. "It was obviously getting to a point where we couldn't continue on the same day-to-day basis," explains Jem. "We knew that we had to get someone in to manage us, and we

wanted someone who was sympathetic."

Remembering a conversation from a couple of weeks before, Finer asked Shane if he had ever met Frank Murray. MacGowan replied that he had and that he liked him and, a few days later, The Pogues gave Murray a call.

Drimnagh CBS is a repressive Christian Brother school set in an old castle on Dublin's South Side. And it was there, during the early sixties, that Frank Murray developed a taste for fast action.

During severe bouts of boredom, Murray and his side-kick Paul Scully would ditch classes and head for a gypsy campsite on the surrounding fields of Ballyfermont. Then, having thieved the sharpest horses they could lay their hands on, they would ride past Drimnagh Castle and wave to the dumb-struck teachers.

Murray's school holidays were invariably spent in Carlow, where – as a 13-year-old – he was involved in pig smuggling. "This guy would drive the pigs in his van, and I'd end up at the border smuggling them across to people on the other side. It was all to do with British bacon subsidies, and this particular guy was making a lot of money. I was only a kid, so it was just a good adventure."

At 15, Murray and Scully were freed from Drimnagh and sent to the more humane confines of Rathmines College Of Commerce where they enrolled for business studies. A greater interest, however, was music: particularly Elvis Presley, blues, and Tamla Motown. They hung out at local hops and, in 1967, witnessed The Black Eagles, a band fronted by the 16-year-old Philip Lynott.

They often skived college in favour of Black Eagles rehearsals in an old school on the Crumlin Road. They travelled to all the band's gigs, and spent much of the rest of their time at Philip's house listening to blues records.

The following year, Lynott joined Skid Row and asked Frank and Paul to roadie. But after a series of gigs around Ireland, Frank decided to quit. "I left Skid Row because they weren't show-ing any signs of moving to England. I wasn't paid the best money to roadie with a part-time band, so I knew I had to get out of the city and get a job or otherwise I'd just continue doing it and never be able to break away."

Scully was equally disgruntled, so they hit London where Frank found work with a computer company and Paul in a clothing firm. But, by 1970, Skid Row had signed a record deal with CBS and, although Lynott had left to start his own band, Murray, Scully and Ted Carroll (who went on to run Chiswick Records) were invited to become professional roadies. The three of them shared a house in the East End and toured England, Germany, Scandinavia and the United States with Skid Row.

"We got our first taste of big time stuff in America," says Frank. "We played the Fillmore West in San Francisco and the Whiskey-A-Go-Go in Los Angeles, and after that you're kind of hooked on that sort of lifestyle – it gets into your system or whatever."

Prior to Skid Row's second tour of the United States, Frank decided to call it a day. By this time he had moved from the East End of London to Hampstead where he shared a large house on Belsize Avenue with Scully, Carroll and various Irish musicians. Among the many habitués of the house was Terry Woods, a former member of Steeleye Span who was, at the beginning of 1972, forming a new band with his wife Gay. And so, on leaving Skid Row, Frank became a sound engineer for The Woods Band.

After tours of England, Denmark, Holland and Ireland The Woods Band split, and Murray re-settled in Dublin where he found work in a record factory, pressing discs. Then, in 1973, having hit the charts with the traditional song 'Whiskey In The Jar', Thin Lizzy (now based in London) toured their native Ireland. "Philip always stayed with me when he came home," says Frank, "and he invited me to go on the road as tour manager-cum-personal manager. I was asked if I had a driving licence so I went out, did my test, and went to London to work with them."

That May, Murray married his schoolday amour Ferga, and Lynott was best man at their wedding. But, not long afterwards, guitarist Eric Bell left the band and Thin Lizzy went off the road. During the lull, Frank learned that Dubliners' manager Noel Pearson had set himself up as a theatrical producer and was looking for a production manager. He immediately returned to Dublin, got the job, and worked on a show titled *Jacques Brel Is Alive And Well And Living In Paris*. Over the next nine months, Murray managed several other productions including *Jesus Christ Superstar*, *Joseph And His Amazing Technicolour Dreamcoat* and *West Side Story*.

In the meantime, Thin Lizzy had recruited Scott Gorham and Brian Robertson and, in the spring of 1976, released 'Jailbreak'. The band lined up a headline tour to promote their LP, and asked Frank to resume his former position. He agreed, and tour managed them through a vintage period which included the hit singles 'Waiting For An Alibi' and 'Don't Believe A Word' and culminated in the 1978 double LP 'Live And Dangerous'.

From there, Murray went on to tour manage for Straight Music, where his charges included The Commodores, Blue Oyster Cult and The Tubes. He was later given the opportunity to open up The Electric Ballroom in Camden Town which was being changed from an Irish ballroom into a rock venue.

"I got some of The Pistols and Thin Lizzy together for the opening," he says. "They called themselves The Greedy Bastards, and it was a great night. I also got Sid Vicious to do a one-off gig with the Vicious White Kids. There was Rat Scabies and, ironically enough, Glen Matlock on bass while Sid sang, and Nancy squealed into the mike like a bad dose of feedback. Unfortunately, that was Sid's last gig in England, shortly after that he went off to America and never returned."

Murray inevitably had trouble with the ballroom over soundproofing and within a year noise complaints had forced the venue to close. He subsequently tour managed for Elton John on

Frank Murray

his comeback dates, working with him through-out Europe but – after a disagreement with Elton's manager – the liaison ended in Glasgow. This disgruntled Murray no end, since it was on the eve of their visit to Moscow.

A lean period followed until he bumped into Rick Rogers in their Camden local, The Devon-shire Arms. Rogers was managing The Specials, who were starting to break big and consequently needed a tour manager. "So I worked on the 2-Tone tour with The Specials, The Selector, Madness and Dexys. Then I tried to work with The Bodysnatchers, but it was very frustrating. They were young, and weren't the kind of band who'd let somebody manage them."

Meanwhile, Kirsty MacColl had asked Frank to manage her. Hearing a tape of 'There's A Guy Works Down The Chip Shop Swears He's Elvis', Murray clicked: "That's a hit." He quickly accepted her offer, and watched the single go Top 20.

By November 1984, he had added songwriter/producer and former Radiator From Space, Philip Chevron to his books. Chevron had recently produced the début single for The Men They Couldn't Hang, and they were the band that Murray was thinking of managing when he was invited to meet The Pogues.

The meeting took place in The Dublin Castle on Camden's Parkway and it was mutually agreed that, from then on, Frank Murray would manage The Pogues.

"I'd had a meeting with The Men They Couldn't Hang a few days before," says Frank, "and I've often thought back but I just can't remember why I made the conscious decision to manage The Pogues. I didn't weigh the talent but, I suppose, I weighed the attitude. The Pogues seemed more open and honest. That's not to say that the others weren't, but they came across like a band who would have to have a meeting about every decision you were going to make.

"I don't think that a band should assume that whatever comes out of a manager's mouth is gospel but if you have a certain relationship, and they know your character, then they should allow you to get on with managing them without look-ing over their shoulder all the time."

rum, sodomy and the cash

Fame might be fleeting, but obscurity lasts a lifetime – and The Pogues knew it. Frank Murray quickly resolved that they would play in any and every venue where people would hand over the money to listen. It was a policy that would pay off dividends in the long term.

"The most important thing was to get them out of London," says Frank. "Everybody knew them on that circuit; they were packing out the pubs, and starting to fill places like the Mean Fiddler. Now the next step was to get them an agent and play around the rest of the country."

Murray's live régime began with the already arranged Lock Up Your Drinks Cabinet Tour. Most of the dates were centred around London but the trail started, on December 5 1984, at Warwick University. Simultaneously, The Pogues hit the airwaves with their second John Peel session. This time they managed to get four tracks past the BBC censors: the traditional 'Whiskey You're The Devil' and 'Danny Boy'; a new song from MacGowan titled 'Sally MacLennane'; and 'Navigator', the slow ballad penned by Phil Gaston.

The Pogues heralded the new year with a headline spot at Harp Lager's ICA Rock Week where, alongside The Sid Presley Experience and Terry And Gerry, they were considered to be among 1985's brightest prospects. End of year honours came from the *NME* poll, with the critics placing 'Red Roses For Me' at number 11, and the readers later voting them as one of the best new bands. But it was John Peel who said it all, when he proclaimed them the finest soul act of 1984. In January, their national assault began in earnest: they were featured on *The Tube* on Friday 11 and spent the next five weeks on the road.

Throughout the month, there were persistent rumours that Elvis Costello wanted to produce the band. Murray telephoned Costello's manager, Jake Riviera, who confirmed that Elvis would be interested in doing a couple of tracks and the party subsequently took to Elephant Studios to record 'A Pair Of Brown Eyes' and 'Sally MacLennane'.

While they were laying down the backing tracks, Costello took Murray to one side, telling him that he really liked what he had heard, and could he produce the next LP? The Pogues immediately consented.

Meanwhile, they had stumbled across the perfect visual complement in film director Alex Cox. Cox had been in London for the opening of his highly acclaimed first feature film, *Repo Man*, and was asked, by *City Limits* reporter Sean Cubbett, if he had seen The Pogues. Although the director replied that he had never even heard of them, in the published article Cubbett managed to transplant his own enthusiasm for the band into Cox's mouth.

Cox consequently received a call from Frank Murray, thanking him for the free plug. When he admitted that, actually, he had never heard The Pogues, Murray sent him a copy of 'Red Roses For Me' and invited him to direct a video for their next single 'A Pair Of Brown Eyes'.

"I thought the album was the most exciting thing I'd heard since punk days," says Alex, "although obviously it was very different. And I thought, you know, I don't wanna do a video but I liked the record so much and I thought there was something about them that would make it worthwhile."

He agreed to shoot the video, and was invited to meet the band when they played in his native Liverpool. "I'd never met any of The Pogues in my life, but, as I came out of Lime Street Station, I saw two guys and thought, these have to be Pogues. So I went up and said, 'Are you Pogues?' and, sure enough, it was Shane and Spider."

Spider quickly dispensed with introductions by saying, "'Ere, is there anywhere we can drink all day long?"

Suitably impressed by that night's show at Liverpool Polytechnic, Cox caught them again, on January 30, at London's Mean Fiddler. "I thought they were excellent," says Alex, "and they'd got such an enthusiastic throng. There were people stage-diving and jumping around and although I'd seen that reaction to American hardcore bands, I'd never seen it happen in England before. And when a band's got a following of people who love them that much and get that

turned on by them, then it's evidence that they've got some kind of magic that other bands don't have."

February brought their first date in Scotland. "We played at Queen Margaret's Hall in Glasgow and it was brilliant; the best gig we'd ever done," enthuses Spider. "I think the Glasgow audience is the greatest in the world."

The band were also given a fleeting four-date view of Ireland: kicking off in Belfast, they rolled through Letterkenny and Cavan before breathing new life into the spirit of Paddy O'Brien in Dublin. Since the Costello tour, The Pogues had attracted considerable attention from the Irish press and their Dublin show was coupled with an early morning TV appearance on *Anything Goes*.

Witnessing The Pogues for the first time in the sweat soaked box that became McGonagles was Murray's old friend, Paul Scully. "It was a very small club and they went down a storm; the atmosphere was really incredible," he says. "Musically, I didn't have a clue what was going on. If you live in Ireland you get used to traditional music, and they were well below that standard. But there was definitely something about them, although I wasn't sure what it was. I went back to Powers' Hotel, met up with Jem and James, and ended up getting thrown out because I wasn't a resident!"

Back home, The Pogues lined up a 20-date tour to coincide with the release of their third single. Written by MacGowan, 'A Pair Of Brown Eyes' is a classic tale of love and drink and death; purple poetry set in the lilt of an accordion sea: 'In blood and death 'neath a screaming sky/I lay down on the ground and the arms and legs of other men were scattered all around . . . / I saw the streams, the rolling hills / where his brown eyes were waiting and I thought about a pair of brown eyes that waited once for me.'

It was backed with the trad song 'Muirshin Durkin' and their latest eulogy to the water of life 'Whiskey You're The Devil'. Both tracks were produced, not in ideal circumstances by Philip Chevron. "We had to get everything done in one day," he says. "But there had been a big party the night before so everyone wandered into the studio like zombies, and there was a very low key atmosphere about the whole thing."

During their January dates it had become clear that, rather than just having Darryl at the mixing desk, The Pogues needed a professional sound engineer. And so, before embarking on their first headline tour, Murray sent for Paul Scully, his friend from the days of Skid Row.

After leaving Skid Row in 1972, Paul had moved to London and worked with The Sutherland Brothers and a series of Irish bands including Grannies Intentions and The Woods Band. He later teamed up with Donovan in County Kildare before quitting the music business for an "aesthetic" life.

In 1981 he started working for a Dublin PA company, but his basic wage was dependent upon painting and carpentry in February 1985, when he first ran into The Pogues at McGonagles. Three weeks later he received an unexpected call from Murray who told him: "There's a ticket for you at the airport."

Paul caught up with the band in Leeds and did his first gig, on March 6 1985, at Nottingham's Rock City. "The thing that clicked with me was definitely the people," he says. "I'd worked with loads of bands, and some bands are just bands first, people second, but it was definitely the crack with these guys. The main thing was you didn't get treated like a roadie. There was no separation between crew and band; no arrogance."

The tour continued for the next three weeks but, headliners though they were, the shows were characterized by hired PAs and 10 bulbs for a lightshow. The climax came with a Saint Patrick's Day celebration at Hammersmith's cramped Clarendon. Elvis Costello warmed the crowd with 'A Man Can Be A Drunk (But A Drunk Can't Be A Man)', and the band took the stage to an un-

Paul Scully

53

paralleled pitch of green. As 'The Auld Triangle' echoed into ribald chants of 'Celtic', The Pogues era had, quite clearly, arrived.

In line with their increasing public profile came a series of interviews – most of them centering on the ubiquitous gargle. *The Face*'s Robert Elms took Shane and Spider on an expenses paid trip from Cricklewood's Crown to Kilburn's National Ballroom and, before long, news of their Bacchanalian exploits even crossed the Atlantic. The Mexican bar band Los Lobos – who had been around for years but were suddenly enjoying similar exposure in the States, and weren't exactly pioneers themselves – asked the *NME* if The Pogues were really drunk all the time.

By the last week of their tour, the band would have had difficulty in disproving such a notion. They degenerated into an all-time stupor at Hull Tiffany's, on March 25, after being subject to the unlimited generosity of Nick Stewart – a Glaswegian whom they had first encountered at Manchester Hacienda just three weeks before.

Being a terminal fan of John Lee Hooker, Howlin' Wolf, The Velvet Underground and Tom Waits, Nick felt an immediate affinity for The Pogues. And, on arriving in Hull, himself and his two companions quickly included the band in their round.

Consequently, by the time The Pogues went on, they were all but legless. Nevertheless, Stewart and Co continued to punctuate their set with one tray after another and, come midnight, they had drunk the house out of both tequila and kitsch.

"Hull's a hellish place," laughs Nick, "and it was a huge hall with only about 150 people there to see them. They were totally wrecked on stage, but they just about managed to perform."

After the show, while the Scots staggered through the streets of Humberside, The Pogues were poured into their transit and ferried southward.

Back in London – where 'A Pair Of Brown Eyes' was enjoying critical fervour and mass cries

of 'hit' – The Pogues worked out an accompanying video with Alex Cox and his co-director Martin Turner.

The result was not exactly standard Stiff stuff: the elusive brown eyes were seen in a paper bag and on a pool cue before being gobbled by a bull dog. Other shots clipped a dull-brained Costello, complete with chest-expander, and The Pogues causing certain controversy by spitting at a poster of Thatcher.

"I'd just seen the film *1984* and been really disappointed by it," says Cox. "There had been so many interesting parallels between Orwell's portrayal and the real 1984 and Thatcher's Britain, but the guys who made that film missed all their opportunities to comment. So 'A Pair Of Brown Eyes' gave us the chance to rant and rave about the fact that we are just Airstrip One for the Americans and their B52 bombers and their Cruise missiles, but everyone is so plugged into their television set or their Sony Walkman that they completely miss out on a global perspective."

Super Stiff, Dave Robinson persuaded Cox and Turner to shoot an alternative to the spitting sequence and, naturally enough, it was the second version which was deemed suitable

The Pogues were given an all too rare chance of plugging the single on the radio by guesting on *Saturday Live*. Andy Batten-Foster freely subjected himself to their caustic humour when he pointed out that Irish rebel songs were more than a yell away from punk. As Spider curled a ready lip to reply "Yeah," pause, "you're right," the airwaves couldn't contain Shane's excessive laugh. Unperturbed as only a Radio One DJ could be, Batten-Foster inquired if they were secret Irish folkies before giving them the go ahead for 'Streams Of Whiskey' and 'A Pair Of Brown Eyes'.

Simultaneously, Cait's velvet voiced sighs were earning widespread acclaim following the release of 'Tommy's Blue Valentine', the first (and last) single from the defunct Pride Of The Cross.

By the middle of April, The Pogues were set for

their first European dates. But, because Marcia was expecting the Finer's second child at roughly the same time, they had to find a temporary replacement for Jem.

Frank happened to mention this to Philip Chevron over a drink in The Devonshire and, even though he had never played banjo in his life, Philip immediately said, "I'll do it." The band agreed that he was worth a chance and, a few days later, Chevron flew as a part-time Pogue to Germany.

Philip Chevron was born Philip Ryan in Dublin, on June 17 1957. His mother, whose maiden name was La Grue, had descended from a French Huguenot family but was a Southside Dubliner of several generations past. His father came from an archetypal Northside Dublin background, and had been an actor and producer before abandoning theatre for the financial security of catering management.

Not surprisingly, Philip was reared on show music. "I listened to 'My Fair Lady', 'Camelot'; everything. I was a big Julie Andrews fan – that was

the first autograph I ever got. When I was a kid I used to go to the Gaiety Theatre in Dublin to see Maureen Potter and Jimmy O'Dea in pantomimes. Jimmy O'Dea was to Ireland what Charlie Chaplin was to Britain: a genuine genius comedian. He made 78 records, and that was the sort of thing I was brought up on."

When Philip was 16, and still studying for his Leaving Cert, he heard Agnes Bernelle (a Berlin-born cabaret singer) on the radio. "I thought, 'This is wonderful'. There was nobody doing anything like that in the world much less in Ireland, and here she is practically living up the road. So I sought her out and introduced myself saying, 'Look I think we should make a record. How are we going to go about it?'" It transpired that Agnes had just made a film, independently of her one-woman Brecht-Weill show, for which a soundtrack had been recorded. So Philip ended up working with her to produce a 12-track LP titled 'Bernelle On Brecht And . . .'

Philip's perspective of the Dublin music scene was garnered from a weekly column, in *The*

55

Evening Press, by Fachtna O'Kelly (who subsequently managed The Boomtown Rats). It was through reading O'Kelly that Philip met like-minded souls Pete Holidai and Steve Rapid and, with the bassist and drummer that he'd recruited for his own band, they formed The Radiators From Space.

The Radiators reached number 17 in the Irish charts with their first single 'Television Screen'. Then, in June 1977, they organized a punk festival in Dublin with Revolver, The Vipers, The Undertones and The Gamblers. Tragically, a fan was stabbed to death during the afternoon and consequently the Radiators found it very difficult to get gigs in Ireland.

They moved to London and in the middle of 1978, directed their energy into a second LP, 'Ghostown' which was produced by Tony Visconti and included the all-time classic 'Faithful Departed'. For various business reasons, 'Ghostown' did not appear until a year after it was recorded and effectively lost its impact.

"The whole thing was really soul destroying. We couldn't even play live 'cos we couldn't afford to. So we were forced to just retreat into the studio and make ever-more ludicrously overproduced records in an attempt to get played on radio. The last couple of singles were all production; studio rubbish. Our heart had gone out of it."

Shortly afterwards, Philip managed to find employment in Camden's Rock On record store. "It was a very good job, 'cos it was an oldies record shop and introduced me to music that up to that point I only knew something about: r 'n' b, soul, country, western swing, cajun. So it was educational, the people who worked there were very good and I was allowed the freedom to take as much time off as I wanted."

Having already produced a single for The Atrix and Agnes Bernelle, it was logical to release a five-track mini LP of Bertolt Brecht and Kurt Weill songs, which appeared towards the end of the year, as 'Songs From Bill's Dancehall'. "Around the same time I produced The Atrix album, alongside Midge Ure and John Leckie. I also played a couple of times at the Stadium in Dublin with Moving Hearts, doing my Brecht-Weill show – which didn't go down terribly well with the audience. And all these things led into producing more records."

In the summer of 1983, Philip decided to record 'The Captains And The Kings' which Brendan Behan had written for his play *The Hostage*. "I knew that it wouldn't be easy to convince record companies about the idea but, having heard 'Shipbuilding' and 'Pills And Soap' by Elvis Costello, I thought that he would probably be sympathetic and definitely wanted him to produce it. I knew Elvis was a customer in Rock On and spoke to him there; he was interested and I sent him a demo. The next day he phoned me and said, 'Let's make a record'.

'The Captains And The Kings' appeared on IMP – the label that Costello created to release his 'Pills And Soap' single with the June General Election – and was backed with 'Faithful Departed' (a song which has since been recorded by both Moving Hearts and Christy Moore).

Philip's next move was asking Frank Murray to manage him. "God knows he had very little to do. I was hardly prolific, so he was managing a record producer more than a performer.

The following year, Chevron drew The Men They Couldn't Hang to Costello's attention and ended up producing their début single 'Green Fields Of France', as IMP's third release. By the spring of 1985, the label's first LP had materialized via Agnes Bernelle's 'Father's Lying Dead On The Ironing Board' – also produced by Philip Chevron.

Although Philip's services had been secured for the whole tour, Jem flew across for The Pogues' opening date at the Alabama Halle in Munich.

Most of the band spent their first afternoon in a comfortable restaurant, knocking back

Philip Chevron

Liebfraumilch, and throwing out possible monik-ers for their next LP. All of a sudden, Andrew piped up with "Rum, sodomy and the lash!" – Churchill's famous synopsis of naval life. There could be no better title.

It was during the same conversation that Frank casually mentioned that The Pogues should be extended into a seven-piece to include his good friend, the reputed Irish folk musician – and former member of Steeleye Span – Terry Woods.

"I thought that the band needed an anchor-man," says Murray, "and I tried to think of somebody who'd fit in with the rest of the person-nel. I was always a great admirer of Terry's, besides the fact that he is a very close personal friend, so I mentioned him to the band. Shane knew of him and of what he'd done, but the name didn't ring a bell with the others."

Back at their hotel, they settled into Murray's room and saw off another crate-load before laun-ching into an accompanied singing session. Later, they decided that now was as good a time as any to introduce themselves to their German tour mana-ger. He turned out to be a sensitive soul named Dirk, and – if he was taken aback by the degener-acy of their appearance – then the best was yet to come.

Their German début, which was to be broad-cast live on TV, was an unmitigated success. "I was more nervous than the band," admits Murray. "In the dressing room I had butterflies in my stomach – I really had. But, by the second number, the heads started to bob and then shoulders went up and you could see that the audience was getting the feel of it. And it was, 'Bang! We have them', and I just relaxed immediately."

Philip Chevron first appeared as a Pogue on their second night, in Stuttgart. "It felt right from the very beginning for them and for me," he says. "It just seemed like I fitted in." Equally sponta-neous was the crazed enthusiasm of the German crowd: yip ey aying with all their madcap might. Poguespeak was – as Munich had hinted – a

language that knew no borders.

The band travelled through Germany in a time-honoured Transit, which had been driven across by Darryl. Lit by the novelty of the occasion, they soon adopted a native accent: their broken English rarely transcending beyond 'alkohol'. Shane's ability to refuel proved incredible even by MacGowan standards and he went without sleep for most of the 10-day trip. "Shane was on great form," says Darryl. "He was completely out to lunch but performing really well."

The Pogues hit Berlin on April 20, Adolf Hitler's birthday. Their appearance at The Loft was, all too predictably, marred by a bunch of boneheads shouting "Sieg heil!" The indomitable Cait launched into a verbal battle while Philip Chevron, adopting the role of MC, left the audi-ence in no doubt about the band's views on Nazis. Minutes later the mindless rant was drowned in the anti-war sentiments of 'Waltzing Matilda', and the appreciative cheers of the majority.

The following morning half the party decided on a token trip to East Berlin. As they ate breakfast in the genteel company of German tourists, in wandered the sleepless Shane. A barefooted, Ray-Banned figure, clad in excessively stained black, pseudo deutsch spieling from his mucained mouth – he was an unforgettable sight.

Later that day, they headed for the lively port of Hamburg and were joined by Uncle Brian, better known as Elvis Costello, who had become increas-ingly inseparable from the band and, more specifi-cally, Caitlin O'Riordan. Cait's impressions of Germany were, by this time, sour and not just because of the night before. "Germany's barmy, full of really fucked up people," she said. "You could have excused it in Berlin because there was a reason, but it was all over the place. I hated it."

Headcases or not, The Pogues played to a packed Hamburg house, and received yet another rip-roaring response. They celebrated in a bar which bordered the Reeperbahn and was run by a man from the town of Dungannon.

Unbeknown to everybody else, Shane, who was last seen passing out in the hotel lobby, ended the night in a nearby hospital. He appeared the next morning with a painfully swollen jaw, saying that he'd "fallen over". When the MacGowan memory failed to account for his fractured cheekbone in any other way, several theories were put forward. They centred on a thorough beating from either the German police, a night porter or persons unknown.

"What we reckon happened," says Spider, "was that the night porter thought he was someone who'd just wandered in, and tried to turf him out. And when Shane attempted to explain that he was a guest the porter didn't want to know, and laid into him."

Their first post-German date was a Greater London Council 'Jobs For Youth' benefit at The Dominion Theatre, alongside The Boothill Foottappers and electric folk hero Richard Thompson. A discernible section of the crowd had paid purely for the pleasure of The Pogues and, as The Foottappers went off, it was obvious that stage precautions weren't what they should be.

"We said that we needed proper security but no one took us seriously," says Jem. "So about 50 people jumped on stage and were dancing around and going mad."

The Pogues played on regardless but, as they finished their set, an over-zealous fan grabbed the mike and shouted: "Who the fuck is Richard Thompson anyway?" This sparked off a terrace chant of "Richard Thompson, Richard Thompson, who the fuckin' hell are you?"

"And the poor bastard was in the dressing room trying to psyche himself up to go on stage," continues Jem. "I don't think he went off us, but it was the last time he wanted us to support him."

Although Thompson's performance passed without incident, The Pogues were suddenly hot news on Fleet Street's brightest pop page. "It was a total riot," a *Daily Mirror* Club reader was reported as saying. "The Pogues seemed to be pretty far gone themselves and they started shouting things to the audience like: 'If anyone is sitting down pour whiskey over them and set them on fire'." The band were horrified at such wanton disregard for whiskey but the Dominion brought further notoriety, and the realization that they didn't need to support anyone in London.

They retired into Elephant Studios to work on 'Rum, Sodomy And The Lash' with Costello at the controls and live engineer Paul Scully, and Nick Robbins, at his side. And, the following week, they set off for the sobriety of Scandinavia. Jem stayed with Marcia so once again Philip Chevron stood in on banjo.

Their route was economy planned, taking them cross channel via Germany to Finland. Boarding the ferry at Travemünde, a seaside resort not far from Lübeck, they spent the next 36 hours on a "very special sailing experience" (© DFDS Seaways) across the Baltic Sea.

Giving the sauna a miss, they settled into the nearest bar. Spider, already banjaxed from the long drive, sprawled himself comfortable and fell

asleep. Two minutes later he was slapped upright by a Finnjet vigilante, and only the unassailable Stacy charm saved him from a night in the brig. But, for the rest of the journey, he was shadowed by the strangely affable Finn. Everywhere Spider went his 'minder' would follow, politely warning him: "Don't drink so much."

Their berths were, as feared, down in the ship's bowels, and by the second night the trip had turned into a nightmare. There was one escape: the devil's brew. "The trouble was," says Andrew, "the only thing we could afford to drink was schnapps."

Fearnley and Chevron entered into a heavy session, with Philip downing a full bottle of the potent liquor. The effect on his stomach ulcer was almost fatal.

"Andrew and Shane had to run up to the bridge to tell the Captain that Philip was dying," recounts Spider. "I was really worried because I didn't want to be left in a cabin with a corpse!"

"And I wouldn't let him smoke," interjects Philip. "Yeah, I kept having to go half out of the door and smoke in the corridor, but keep looking back to make sure he was still breathing. And if he stopped breathing I didn't know what I was supposed to do, because how do you give someone mouth to mouth resuscitation when they've died because of something that's wrong with their stomach?" asks Stacy. "Fortunately he's still here, but his first experience of Finland was a Finnish hospital."

Freed at last from the floating hell of the Finnjet Ferry, the rest of the band were set upon by Customs. "They had a sniffer dog, looking for drugs or explosives or whatever," says Spider. "But all it was interested in was the seat of Shane's pants."

"It kept having a go at my trousers, and it wouldn't leave my socks alone. I don't think they train sniffer dogs very well over there," comments Shane.

As if Finland's restricted licensing laws weren't trial enough, they found themselves ensconced in Helsinki's YMCA, a less than convivial establishment which bore the temperance legend: "No unchristian behaviour will be tolerated here."

Sweden and Norway were, by comparison, sanctuary. Cait, the sole appreciator of Finland's fjords, was captivated by the Norwegian landscape. "I loved Norway better than anywhere I've ever been; apart from sentimental reasons for Ireland," she says. "The scenery was incredible."

During the Norwegian dates, The Pogues live act peaked new levels of energy. A big part of this was James, leaping around with admirable disregard for his 50 kilo accordion. "Me and Phil were going hell for leather," he explains. "Trying to compete with each other, seeing who could jump the highest, and just really physically enjoying it. That's why I get as active as I do on stage. And also I think it's really good being able to heave one of those fuckers around instead of just having it sit on your chest."

The Norwegians were entranced – not least by Spider, going hog wild on beer tray. An imposing skinhead was particularly fascinated: "Ah! Spider! I have seen you and you are hitting yourself over ze head vit a trombown! No!," he exclaimed, smacking himself in the head with his fist. "I am stupid! It voz a beer barrel!"

Back in London – where Jem was now the father of another daughter, Kitty – they returned to Elephant Studios, and finished recording 'Rum, Sodomy And The Lash'.

Meanwhile Philip Chevron, survivor of two European tours and the Finnjet fiasco, had become inseparable from the band. And because it had been decided that Shane shouldn't play guitar, but focus solely on singing, Philip was deemed the ideal solution.

"It just became gradually obvious in Europe that I wanted to stay and they wanted me to stay if I wanted to," says Philip. "Shane had been not wanting to play guitar for some time, so it seemed logical that when Jem came back I would be the guitarist."

At the beginning of June, The Pogues went back to Ireland. They headlined Whit Weekend at the Cibeal Festival in Kenmare, a picturesque town set among the Kerry hills and backdropped by the lofty heights of the MacGillicuddy Reeks. But, despite the acquisition of Philip Chevron, Frank Murray was still convinced that there was a place in The Pogues for his multi-faceted friend Terry Woods.

"I invited him to meet the band in Kenmare," says Murray, "but because the place was new to them and the weather was beautiful, it was a quick handshake, a 'Hello, Terry' and they were off! So he ended up being left in a room with no one but myself."

Woods did not, however, let their lack of decorum colour his first impressions. "I'd heard tapes and read reviews so I knew what they were about and what they were into. I think MacGowan is a great writer, and when I saw them I could see that they were taking parts of Irish music into a direction which it needs to go in. It's become

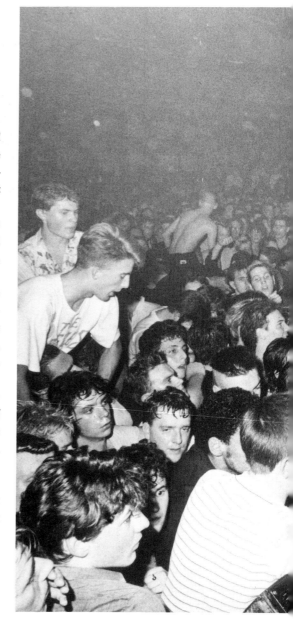

too insular."

The Pogues' raucous set was generally regarded as the highlight of the festival; although their artistic intent was questioned by Ireland's more delicate sensibilities. A stocious Shane managed to throw up over Cait's amp, while Spider did likewise in Rosslare. "He threw up all over his suit and had to leave it in a bin," laughs Shane. "That was his present to Mother Ireland."

The following Tuesday they made their live début on the BBC's *Whistle Test*. Jem hadn't travelled to Kenmare, so it was their first time as a seven-piece. "It was a live appearance at 10 o'clock in the morning," remembers Philip, "and it was

really strange because there was this extra person on stage who was quite foreign to me, and it must have been just as odd for Jem. Still we do tend to throw ourselves in at the deep end sometimes."

Severe stomach pains had, by this stage, forced Shane to think about his long suffering liver. He eventually gave in to medical advice and took the hitherto inconceivable measure of giving up whiskey. "Shortening my life doesn't worry me," he says. "I just don't like the way it makes me feel. I kept drinking more whiskey to make me feel better, which it does for a while, and then you get to feel even worse." MacGowan replaced the sacred spirit with white wine.

On June 9, Barry McGuigan boxed his way into the World Featherweight title and, suddenly, everyone was sprouting shamrocks. The Pogues couldn't have timed their fourth single better.

The upfront ring of mandolin, tin whistle and accordion, and the infectious refrain of 'far away' made MacGowan's 'Sally MacLennane' a supreme stomper and new hymn for the exile. Its Celtic flavour hung over to the B-side with rough cuts of 'The Wild Rover' and 'The Leaving Of Liverpool'. But, like 'A Pair Of Brown Eyes' (which had reached the Top 70), 'Sally MacLennane' suffered through an absence of daytime radio play. The talk of 'whores' didn't increase its BBC potential, and

it peaked at Number 50 before fading out.

Simultaneously, they made another round of England and Scotland, rapidly earning a reputation for the hottest live act in the country. Their following seemed to grow with every gig, and invariably included a hardcore of Celtic supporters who had tied the Pogue flag to their own.

Their treks continued into a spate of outdoor festivals, beginning on mid-summer day at Glastonbury, where they shone through a quagmire of mud. Backstage, Frank Murray met up with The Boomtown Rats' enduring lightsman, and pal of his Dublin days, Paul Verner. Verner – who had previously worked with Skid Row, Thin Lizzy and Horslips – knew that The Rats would be off the road for winter, so dispensed with formalities by saying, "Gis a job". Murray promised to give him a call.

A couple of weeks later The Pogues were billed, appropriately enough, for the Hood Festival in Devon. And, on July 7, they reached their widest audience ever before 80,000 at the GLC's 'Jobs For A Change' red letter day in Battersea Park. By the time they got to WOMAD, their audience had taken on a cross-cultural identity of its own: from punks, football supporters, psychobillies, students and folk fans to anyone with a tint of green blood, all mesmerised by The Pogues' energy and lack of pretension.

The focal point was undoubtedly Shane MacGowan, a man with no style but his own. MacGowan's unconventional looks and stumbling stage presence make him the antithesis of the plastic popstar, while his vivid narratives offer similar doses of rugged realism.

The most notable of these was 'The Old Main Drag', a song almost as old as the band itself, but which they had recently resurrected. Beginning with the line 'When I first came to London, I was only 16,' and sung with the gravel-throated growl that could belong to no one but Shane, it quickly became a favourite with the crowd.

In the meantime, Frank Murray had devised a nautical theme for 'Rum, Sodomy And The Lash', and the band were duly decked in full Napoleonic regalia and photographed at London's Tower Bridge. The LP was wrapped in a Pogue parody of JLA Gericault's macabre painting 'Le Radeau de La Medusa'.

"The history of the painting is exactly the same as a lot of Pogue songs," says Jem. "Lots of our songs are about people being shat on. Not by any particular system but just because people are always shat on. They're not explicitly political but implicitly we're very political."

On July 30, 'Rum, Sodomy And The Lash' was launched on a sea of freebies at the press scam of the year. The grog poured thick and fast as 400 freeloaders piled onto HMS Belfast, moored on the Thames, for The Pogues' coming-out party. Booze bearing sailors wandered the gangplank, while seven scruffy Wellingtons posed as Napoleon and faced Waterloo with a steaming set.

"We were far from sober," admits Spider, "but the state the journalists were in! They were completely langoured by all the free booze."

Melody Maker went conspicuously over the top, over the eight and finally overboard as a sub editor

splashed into the river. The Pogues ended their sublime night of liggin' in the riggin' with a mass knees-up on the quarter-deck and, as the guests made off with their free records, they were unlikely to be disappointed.

Loaded to the gunnels with energy and emotion, 'Rum, Sodomy And The Lash' was among the most essential vinyl of 1985. The cinematic imagery, additional instrumentation and polished production certainly came as a shock to the band's detractors.

Six of the 12 tracks were Pogue originals, all showing MacGowan to be a songwriter of the highest calibre. The scene was familiar – 'The Old Main Drag' delves into the darker, seamy streets of London; its brutal story of alienation rasped at an unusually slow pace: 'And now I am lying here, I've had too much booze/ I've been spat on and shat on and raped and abused/ I know that I'm dying and I wish I could beg for some money to take me from the old main drag.' Tommy Keane's uileann pipes highlight the sleaze and terminal despair.

'Old Main Drag' was untypical of the LP's overall mood. This was summed up by 'The Sick Bed Of Cuchulainn', a glorious rampage through life which left nothing on hedonism unsaid. Similar spirit was reflected in the former single 'Sally MacLennane' which reappeared alongside 'A Pair Of Brown Eyes'. Side one also included the 'Wild Cats Of Kilkenny', a strident ceili punctuated by yelps and shrieks; and Cait's haunting interpretation of 'I'm A Man You Don't Meet Every Day'.

The second side opened with Ewan MacColl's 'Dirty Old Town', a well known ballad, rich in imagery and enhanced by Henry Benagh's fiddle, whose strings were even more to the fore on Spider's uptempo version of 'Jesse James'. The pace slowed into 'Navigator', their trad tale of toil and hardship, written by Phil Gaston (the man behind 'Tommy's Blue Valentine') and followed by 'Billy's Bones' and a blitzing attack on 'The Gentleman Soldier'. The LP faded with an ex-

tended rendition of the Eric Bogle classic 'And The Band Played Waltzing Matilda'. This long-standing favourite from their live set re-echoed the anti-war views of 'Brown Eyes' and so succinctly heard on MacGowan's 'Billy's Bones': 'Now Billy's out there in the desert sun and his mother cries when the morning comes/ and there's mothers cryin' all over this world for their poor dead darlin' boys and girls.'

Like 'Red Roses' before it, 'Rum, Sodomy And The Lash' managed to capture both the joy and despair of everyday life. Much ado was made of the latter. At least eight of the 12 tracks refer, at some point, to death, as the press were quick to point out.

"How can you possibly look at life without thinking about death? How can you possibly put life into any kind of reasonable perspective without death being on the border of it?" demands Shane, less saturnine than his lyrics. "The songs are not about death; they're about life."

'The Sick Bed Of Cuchulainn' illustrated his point. It could be analysed as yet another song about death and destruction but is in fact the ultimate celebration of life: 'They'll take you to Cloughprior and shove you in the ground, but you stick your head back out and shout, 'We'll have another round'.'

MacGowan evaded thematic analysis by dismissing his work as songs in the pitch of life. "The songs are all based around fairly basic street level existence in London, which is the life that I've led most of my life," he explains. "I used to stay at my uncle's pub which is where 'Sally MacLennane' comes from. I also spent a lot of time down the 'dilly when I was teenager, which is where 'The Old Main Drag' comes from. It isn't necessarily about me . . . it's what I saw. All the rest of it is just stuff that, if you spend a lot of time living the – I don't know the word for it – *real* life in central London, you see it or it happens to you. I've worked in pubs and done other shit jobs, it's just that I've observed and remembered it, or it

affected me enough to write about it. Not affected me so that I wanted to say any great message about it, just that I like thinking about things and then writing about them. I don't like writing about my own personal hang ups which is what a lot of other populists do, I just like giving an impression of real life."

Shane's impressions proved a little too real for Woolworths. The chain store insisted that all copies of 'Rum, Sodomy And The Lash' be stamped with the warning: "Contains language that might be considered offensive".

And while the record was generally soaked in lavish superlatives, The Pogues were criticized for macho overtones of the lyrics. Their version of 'The Gentleman Soldier' was, for example, imbued with as clear a Slide It In mentality as any Whitesnake song.

"People get very oversensitive," says Philip Chevron. "They read attitudes into things that aren't there. You look at Shane and there isn't any of that heavy metal macho bullshit in him at all. In fact he is – in the old fashioned sense of the word – a perfect gentleman; a scholar and a gentleman.

"And if I, in all honesty, thought that 'Transmetropolitan' was offensive then I wouldn't be in this group. What's the line? 'We'll scare the Camden Palace poufs and worry all the whores' and the bit about 'the queers from the GLC'. I mean, I'm a faggot and I'm not offended. It would be ludicrous to be offended, and you could level the same accusations from a gay man's point of view as from a militant feminist's or whatever, but you'd be very stupid if you did because there aren't any macho overtones.

"You only have to look at the people that the members of this band share their lives with – the girlfriends and wives – to realize that if any of us were remotely male sexist pigs, then those people wouldn't be our partners. I've got a lot of sympathy with the feminist cause and, of course, the gay cause, without being an Islingtonian about it, but I think that very often there's a sort of inverted

fascism at work, where people go out looking for examples of chauvinism or sexism or racism and see things that aren't there."

If anyone could single-handedly trounce the cries of 'sexism' then it was Cait. "Whose is that voice? Who is that womin?" demanded an excited feminist on hearing 'Tommy's Blue Valentine' at a disco. "Is it some really famous jazz record that I'm just not aware of?"

Minutes later, she recoiled in horror on learning that the same singer was not only a Pogue but also responsible for a track titled 'I'm A Man You Don't Meet Every Day'. "Oh dear," sneered O'Riordan's former admirer. "She's obviously the subject of male domination."

"That's not something that I come up against," comments Cait. "People might say, 'Oh, she's the subject of male domination' but they don't have to come up and say it to my face. They certainly don't say it if they meet me backstage or in an interview. But if anyone ever did try male domination on me, they'd have to be a lot taller than me, a lot bigger than me, and a lot more vicious."

The release of 'Rum, Sodomy And The Lash' was followed by a benefit concert for the Nicaraguan Solidarity Campaign at Brixton Fridge. Organised by Alex Cox and Simi Bedford, the line-up consisted of The Pogues, The Men They Couldn't Hang, The Boothill Foot-tappers and Elvis Costello. Not surprisingly, tickets were in heavy demand and, by the time the doors locked shut, the 2,000 capacity Fridge had overflowed with almost as many more spending the night on the street.

"When the place was full," says Alex Cox, "I walked around the outside and there were 2,000 people waiting to get in, who couldn't. There was this tremendous amount of support for The Pogues, and I was thinking, 'Wow! This is phenomenal'. I felt like Bill Graham!"

Two days later, on August 9, The Pogues took up an engagement of a different kind. They travelled north to Shotts, near Glasgow, at the

behest of Nick Stewart, who had done his utmost to keep them entertained in Hull, and who ran a pub-cum-venue called The Mucky Duck.

Arriving in the early hours of the evening, they drank their way through Friday night and – thanks to the increasing generosity of the locals – repeated the process the following morning.

"No one believed that they were really going to come until they actually arrived," says Nick. "It's a wee venue for 300, and people came down from Stirling and up from Newcastle and, on the Saturday night, there were 300 people inside and 100 outside who couldn'ae get in. It was ridiculous."

Equally ridiculous was the state of Mr Stacy. Spider – who couldn'ae say no to anything – had taken to the free drink like blotting paper: he was hog-wimpering by 6.00 pm, unable to move at 7.00 pm and completely comatose e'er after.

By 10.00 pm the other Pogues, and the accompanying Costello, had tried almost every known method of resuscitation and had no alternative but to leave Stacy's body in the van and, none too sober themselves, do the set without him. The tin-whistle eventually awoke at midnight and asked Shane, in all earnestness, "Were we any good, tonight?"

Good or downright diabolical it made little difference: the atmosphere was something else. After the show, there was a mass call for carryouts – which evolved into a late-night party in a nearby park.

Unfortunately, two policemen chanced by, and – oblivious to the difficulties of moving 100 delirious people – told the gathering to shift. Within minutes the scene was hit by a dozen screaming sirens, 30 policemen and their none too friendly dogs.

"All of a sudden it was like a police state," insists Nick. "There were 34 arrests but every single one of those charges was later dropped – which proves how unnecessary it all was. There were no problems at all: just people having a

bloody good time which, for some obscure reason, had to be curbed."

But, within 12 hours, the atmosphere had re-charged for The Pogues' Sunday night show and, this time, Spider managed to play on stage as well as in his dreams.

"Two nights, and it was just out of this world," says Nick. "They were far too big for our place but they did it 'cos they're such lovely people."

Their departure time was scheduled for an ambitious 1.00 pm on Monday. But one lunchtime pint inevitably led to another and it was 6.00 pm before the van – driven on this occasion by Phil Gaston – eventually pulled away, with a heapful of flutered Pogues scrambling for the windows, screaming their good-byes and, God help everyone, threatening to return.

The following weekend was spent in Austria. Having enjoyed a thunderous reception at Cambridge, in July, The Pogues were lined up for the Vienna Folk Festival alongside Richard Thompson, Tom Verlaine, Fairport Convention, their forefathers The Dubliners and a host of European groups.

The Pogues whole set went down a bomb. "It was a great gig," enthuses Philip. "And it was also very encouraging that at a straight folk festival people abandoned their preconceptions and their bigotry and just enjoyed themselves, which was exactly what had happened at Cambridge before. Although a folk festival in Britain, where you're really well known is one thing, and a folk festival in Vienna quite another."

At home, the LP had climbed into the Top 20, confirming The Pogues growing popularity. It would take more than the BBC play-list to stop them. 'Rum' sales flowed throughout August while the band took a holiday.

Shane headed for the solitude of a Greek Island. "There are three places I've been to that I love, and that's London, Ireland and Greece," he said afterwards, Greek cross around his neck. "The Greek Islands are like Ireland was before they started

building roads all over the place. The people just get on with their fishing and don't give a shit. No one speaks English, it's a brilliant place."

Meanwhile, 'Dirty Old Town' had been released as their fifth single. The flip side carried 'The Parting Glass', a traditional song which they made their own, and 'A Pistol For Paddy Garcia', an instrumental displaying Jem Finer's penchant for spaghetti-westerns. The record was accompanied by an incredibly bland video, shot through a haze of dry ice in the soulful surrounds of Brixton Fridge.

"That video is nothing to do with us," says Jem. "Alex Cox was meant to do it but Frank went on holiday and Dave Robinson stepped in. He decided that Alex Cox wasn't going to do it, because he was too expensive and he made mad and crazy videos that weren't going to sell a record. Robinson just set the whole thing up and it was crap. I wanted them to get lots of people dancing and cut it in, which would have been much more exciting."

Finer was equally contemptuous of the single's sleeve. "The painting on 'Dirty Old Town' is really useless. It's just pathetic. There's so many better impressionistic low-life painters than this person you've never heard of called Ainsworth. Edward Burra for example is just brilliant but that was completely derivative, like some London arsehole trying to be an impressionist. And the lettering on the cover is awful, which is also what happened on 'Rum, Sodomy And The Lash'. The 'Sodomy' was all very sensational, when it's not trying to be gauche or clever saying, 'Rum, Sodomy And The Lash' ha! ha! What a controversial title! It has a bearing on the whole of the record and the feeling of the songs. But the lettering really cheapened it."

Despite its handicaps, everyone expected 'Dirty Old Town' to be the band's first hit. It wasn't. But at least it was inoffensive enough to lift the curse of Pogue Mahone. The Pogues were

*Terry
Woods*

played on daytime radio, at last.

Murray sent a copy of 'Rum, Sodomy And The Lash' to 'Dirty Old Town' composer Ewan Mac-Coll, who told him: "I didn't care for 'Dirty Old Town' much at first but I find it sounds better with each hearing. I like the other tracks a lot. Tremendous energy and real honest to God anger. Splendid. Hope the anger doesn't get blunted. Success can be like being trampled to death by tame geese."

With their star swaying in the ascendant, The Pogues hit the road yet again, this time for a 20-date stint, spanning September and ranging from Scunthorpe Park to Hammersmith Palais. The Free Festival in Scunthorpe, on September 1, was Paul Verner's last show with The Boomtown Rats before accepting Frank Murray's promised offer of a job, as The Pogues lighting engineer.

Around the same time Frank Murray sent a telegram to Terry Woods at his home near Virginia, County Cavan, asking him to come to London to join The Pogues.

Born in Dublin, on December 4 1947, Terry Woods' interest in music was originally shaped by his sister May, who is six years his senior. "I was always a bit of a maverick, and couldn't identify with a lot of rock 'n' roll," he says. "I really liked Buddy Holly, Tommy Roe and The Everly Brothers, but I didn't understand why. Then May introduced me to classical music, and she also got involved with the folk scene – which was only just beginning – and she took me along to that. I then discovered that I really liked American country and mountain music, which in turn led me to understand why I like Buddy Holly."

It was then, at 14, that Terry got his first instrument: a five-string banjo. "Being part of the American old-time mountain culture, the five-string banjo really appealed to me."

Terry's girlfriend, Gay, had a brother – confusingly called Terry – who was also drawn to folk music and it wasn't long before he and the Woods had formed their own group. Gay quickly learnt to play guitar, and when May dropped out she joined up. The band was eventually whittled down to just Gay and Terry Woods who, calling themselves The Apprentice Folk (later shortened to The Prentice Folk), played and sang as a duo for the next four years.

It was with Terry's next band, a trio called Sweeney's Men, that he made his first records – the singles 'Waxies Dargle' and 'Sullivan's John' and the 1968 LP 'Sweeney's Men'. And, although 'Sweeney's Men' was only moderately successful, the band was highly influential: pioneering the use of double-stringed instruments like the bouzouki.

When Andy Irvine left the band to travel through Eastern Europe, Woods and Johnny Moynihan experimented with electric music and commandeered a blues guitarist called Henry McCullough.

"He had toured a lot with Hendrix and, at the time, was a very famous guitar player," says Woods, "and when he joined we were really going somewhere electrically. But the record company (Transatlantic) were very reticent, as usual, to put money into the band in order to finance the equipment we needed. Joe Cocker offered Henry a gig with him, and although Henry loved what we were doing, because of the record company's attitude it seemed as if we were going up a blind alley, so he took the gig and subsequently played on all the great Joe Cocker tracks."

Meanwhile, Woods and Moynihan – the surviving but increasingly disillusioned Sweeney's Men – spent most of their time in London. They drank in The Prince Of Wales in Hampstead, a meeting place for many musicians including Fairport Convention. Woods consequently met up with Ashley Hutchings, and they had several discussions about developing the potential of electric folk.

"We were very interested in getting a British/Irish band together on the basis of The Byrds," explains Terry. "And that's basically what we set out to do – and it was nearly successful."

In November 1969, Hutchings left Fairport

Convention and spent the following month rehearsing with Terry and Gay Woods, Johnny Moynihan and Andy Irvine. The latter pair backed out (going on to Planxty, and Moynihan also to De Dannan) but, in January 1970, Hutchings and the Woods recruited Tim Hart and Maddy Prior, and formed Steeleye Span.

They recorded 'Hark! The Village Wait' on RCA but split, after just four months, without playing any gigs. "Unfortunately we began to develop differences within the band," says Terry, "and decided to break up, except that the band didn't actually break up. There was a lot of politics going on, and everybody left supposedly – but in fact it was one of those tricks to get rid of us, although we were the founder members."

While Steeleye Span headed for considerable commercial success, the Woods were approached by Doctor Strangely Strange. They joined somewhat reluctantly – since they had also recorded some demos with Ian McDonald and Michael Giles of King Crimson, and were hoping to further that partnership – but toured with the Strangelys over the following year.

By January 1972, though, Terry had made a conscious decision to form his own band. The result was The Woods Band: a collaboration between Terry, Gay and various musicians. But after tours of England, the Continent and Ireland, the inevitable 'differences' reared and the band split in Holland before finally fizzling in Dublin.

It was at this point that Terry and Gay re-settled in Ireland and reverted to being a duo. With the aid of session musicians, they made extensive tours of Europe and recorded four LPs, the last of which was titled 'Tenderhooks'.

In 1980, Terry and Gay parted company, and Terry immersed himself in a new project: The Woods Band, Mark II. But, as soon as they started recording, Terry realized that the band had been a mistake. "I should have just taken a total and final break. I'd reached a kind of crescendo – between personal problems and the general hassle of being involved in the music business for so long – and just had to get away from it."

Terry eventually calmed down in the Cavan countryside, with his new wife Marian and their children Sarah and Hazel. He had managed to stay away from the music business for almost five years when Frank Murray suddenly suggested that he should join The Pogues. Woods checked them out at Kenmare and, having liked most of what he saw, was keener to make a comeback. "Frank wanted me to go back on the road and I kind of had itchy feet to go back anyway – so The Pogues seemed the perfect opportunity."

Fourteen weeks later, Woods received his summons.

Terry immediately flew to London, and joined The Pogues at their rehearsal room in Tufnell Park. "I told him to come on over and give it a shot," says Frank. "But everybody was very wary. The band rehearsed a set, then Terry got up and tried to play with them, and it was complete chaos – a catastrophe. And yet I knew that, as long as the band were prepared to give him time to break himself in, it was going to happen."

The following day, September 5, Terry was back in Ireland, ready to play cittern and concertina as a special guest Pogue. Their first stop was Dublin, where 'Rum, Sodomy And The Lash' had aroused curiosity to such an extent that their only rival for media attention was the moving statue of Ballinspittle.

Controversy was fuelled when the band were invited to answer questions on an RTE radio show. Hosted by DJ and good vibes specialist BP Fallon, it featured a studio panel of journalists, traditional musicians and fans. With The Pogues on one side, the inquisition on the other and barely a drop of drink between them it was hardly a cordial atmosphere.

Relations deteriorated when a concertina player and former member of Planxty, Noel Hill, attacked the band's musicianship. Hill, whose perception of music began and ended with Seamus Ennis, stated that The Pogues – in common with the "rowdy ballad music" of The Dubliners and Clancy Brothers – were "a terrible abortion" of Irish music.

This led to a discussion, as heated as it was inevitable, about the band's 'Irishness'. Journalist Joe Ambrose made a laudable attempt to quell the point, by saying: "It's said that folk music is the background to us being a proud, independent nation and, if you come from a place like Tipperary – which is where the Clancys come from – you'd probably regard folk music as being more suitable for molesting sheep to. Whereas The Pogues reflect elements of sordidity and earthiness and poverty, which are much more interesting and which have nothing to do with being Irish or English or American."

Noel Hill, however, laboured his case and it was at this stage that Andrew went for an unexpected Grundy, and said: "I think it just comes down to sex. I mean, are you a better fucker than me?" The session continued in similar style for another half hour, and eventually ended with the contemptuous Cait being branded "a pig". She replied with five seconds of suitable snorts.

By this time, the issue of 'tradition' had become a common carp against them. Shane put the record straight: "Tradition is something that has passed from generation to generation. Those of us in the group with Irish backgrounds or who were actually brought up in Ireland must have the Irish tradition in us. We can't be traditional because we don't stick to just what was handed down, but we can't be against tradition because we were built on a tradition. So, therefore, the argument is spurious; it's ridiculous."

Irish purists were not the only back biters. The Pogues were also accused of perpetuating the stereotype of the comical drunken Irish. Joe Breen wrote, in *The Irish Times*, of a black man who had said that he disliked the blues because it reminded

him of the days of virtual slavery; he preferred listening to modern black music. And it was the same for Irishman Breen who considered The Pogues to be a raffish reflection on Oirland's unsophisticated past.

Such notions were given credence by the band's constant allusions to drink, and the sight of Spider bashing his brains out with a beer tray. But it was a view that The Pogues disregarded. "People drink and people don't; it's irrelevant," sighs Shane. "Tom Waits isn't accused of perpetuating drunken stereotypes so why should we be? Okay, so maybe we're real alkies but that's got nothing to do with what we do as a group."

"It doesn't matter what we do in our private lives," says Jem. "The point is that people like us because we provide something that no one else does which is playing straight songs. Most other groups don't play actual songs: you get a Duran Duran record and it's got really good production but the words mean nothing apart from a celebration of the lifestyle that they've attained for themselves. We play songs which deal with subjects that are common to all people regardless of their class

Paul Verner

or their race. They're about feelings that everyone has whether they try and pretend they do or they don't. Songs that you can sing in a bath or sing with a hundred guitarists, and the music is very melodic, with a lot of emotion and soul."

Jem's words were borne out by the way the audience reacted to their Irish dates. Dublin's SFX Centre (aka Saint Francis Xavier's) managed to squeeze over 1500 into its less than spacious confines. The result was a flaming field of heads, scarves, raised arms and tattered Tricolours. The response was repeated the following night at Queen's University, Belfast. Drunken deadbeats or not, the Irish crowds couldn't care less.

Over on Scottish soil, Glasgow's Barrowland Ballroom gave the band their greatest night yet. The unexpected death of Celtic's King had aroused their fans' fervour and the atmosphere resounded with the collective cry, "Jock Stein! Jock Stein!". The Pogues were suddenly playing Parkhead and the Old Firm weren't in sight.

"The Barrowlands crowd are absolute magic," enthuses Spider. "It's the kind of place where the crowd really makes the show, because they're coming across with such fibre, such energy. And it's all really positive as well. I've never detected any malice in any of the gigs we've done in Scotland. It's just people going out and having a really good time, and we pick up and respond to that. The audience makes it and I think that's why people say that Glasgow is such a good gig."

If their stage act wasn't exactly polished, then Paul Verner's lightshow and an intro tape of 'Paddy Garcia' gave presentation a new meaning. Returning to England, the tour shifted into top gear. The Pogues seemed to transcend the barriers of style and subculture: attracting everyone from the curious and the disillusioned to those who were (at least in their own mind's eye) The Boys From The County Hell. "The nearest parallel I can find is a football match," says Cait. "They're the football hooligans and we're Arsenal or something."

It was sold-out signs every other night, with the lucky ones going where spirits took them and singing all the words from 'The Old Main Drag' to 'The Wild Rover'. But it wasn't just a question of the songs – The Pogues were now capable of crowd communication in a way that their contemporaries couldn't approximate. Not only had they added to their repertoire but Terry Woods had further increased their musical prowess. On stage, they possessed an energy and wild shamrock abandon that recalled the most speed scorched punk.

"It all boils down to energy," enthuses Scottish author Iain Banks, "and The Pogues have got it; it's foot stamping music, shouting and yelling and roaring music; drunken Irish bandit music, and the sheer gleeful raucousness of a song like 'Sally MacLennane' just takes my breath away, it also leaves me grinning like an idiot, happy just for hearing it."

Banks – creator of the gloriously psychotic and

critically lauded *The Wasp Factory* – was, at the time, working on a third novel, *The Bridge*, and decided to incorporate The Pogues into one of the central events of the book: a cassette of 'Rum, Sodomy And The Lash' is playing in the principal character's car when he crashes into the rear of another.

"The song which I heard first," says Iain, "and which made me want to buy 'Rum' was 'I'm A Man You Don't Meet Every Day', which I heard on Peelie's show. I loved the song, but I loved the way Cait O'Riordan sang it even more; as though through continual not quite-asleep sighs. It's an amazing (and ambiguously erotic) performance; a brilliant counterpoint to the fiendish power of so many of the other tracks. I suppose that's another reason I'm so enthusiastic. If The Pogues were only the most energetic exponents of Celtic folk-punk, they'd be just another good band, but they have a range of styles and a grasp of emotional resonance that lifts them above that.

"And then there's the politics; left up my street. The Pogues sing for the oppressed and the exploited without being patronising or sentimental, and somehow there's an anarchic, rebellious attitude that comes out even in the songs not obviously about authority and its various uniformed symptoms. Maybe it's just something to do with Shane's voice; it's like a rusty bayonet . . . but I don't think that's all there is to it."

Whatever it was that The Pogues had, the demand for it was increasing, and the weekend of September 20-22 provided Shane with two of his finest moments.

The first came via a trip back to Dublin and an appearance on Gay Byrne's frequently controversial *Late Late Show*. A post-Band Aid Bob Geldof was also appearing that night and offered to introduce them.

It was decided that MacGowan would perform live, while the band mimed. This left Shane with the near impossible task of singing the furious-paced 'Sick Bed' to a backing tape. But technical

hiccups didn't spare RTE viewers from the blasphemous blast: 'They took you up to Midnight Mass and left you in the lurch, so you dropped a button in the plate and spewed up in the church.'

The Pogues were scheduled to return to England the following day but, come lunchtime, there was still no sign of Shane. After much shuffling and waiting around, the band were driven to the airport, and a rescue party was sent through the pubs of Dublin for the rambling singer. Finding no joy in the six likeliest places, the search for MacGowan was all but given up. He was eventually found in the fourteenth bar they checked out and quickly packed off to Folkestone – arriving just in time for that night's gig at Leas Cliff Hall.

The following day brought another high when, on the afternoon of their sold-out show at the Hammersmith Palais, Channel 4 used 'Sally MacLennane' as the trailer for the GAA Cup Final between Dublin and Kerry live from Croke Park. This more than compensated for the fact that the same Channel had simultaneously deemed the band 'too ugly' to appear on its *Bliss* pap programme.

The Pogues celebrated their third birthday, on October 4, at Ipswich's Gaumont Theatre. Coincidentally, Frank Murray's former charges Thin Lizzy had made their Robertson/Gorham début on the same day, eight years before. It was also the feast of Saint Francis of Assisi. Although Shane's carefree ways left him many miles from his 'vision' he was, like Brendan Behan before, already a veritable Francis. The press had long since championed him at the head of the-down-and-outs, with the *NME* stamping The Pogues audience as "the unclean" and declaring MacGowan's 'Transmetropolitan' and 'The Old Main Drag' as "veritable anthems for a generation of squat culture kids". Canonization couldn't be far·off as The Pogues evolved into that paper's pet band. "We're *NME*'s pet band, we're *Sounds*' pet band, we're *Melody Maker's* pet band – we're not anybody's pet band," protested Shane. "We're so popular they

can't ignore us, it's as simple as that."

What's more The Pogues were becoming increasingly multi-lingual; the spirit could be translated into any language. And so, after a futile attempt to record their Christmas single in a few days, they set off on yet another transchannel trip. Since it was to be a four-week round of Holland, France, Germany, Switzerland and Scandinavia, they were afforded the luxury of their first tour bus. Its territorial areas were three-fold: upfront the cinema, at the back the rehearsal room and conveniently centred in the middle was a make-shift bar.

The video screen was invariably filled with Sergio Leone's 220-minute epic *Once Upon A Time In America* obsessively watched, at least once a day,

by Shane and Spider and thus force fed to the choiceless crew. "I went to see that film four times in two weeks," says Shane. "I love things like that: James Cagney, Robert de Niro; good gangster movies. I'm just a frustrated psychopath really." He subsides into the unmistakable MacGowan laugh, a sound which has been described as everything from the crackle of a cheap walkie-talkie to an overheated Buick rattling its last gasp. Whatever, it's a hiss that's been closely copied by Spider and, in Europe, proved infectious. "I must admit that I lapsed into it for a while," says PV (Paul Verner). "But then I thought, Paul, pull yourself together."

The only sound to really overshadow Leone – and Shane 'n' Spider's spin-off grunts of "Hey, pal, how are ya? Good to see ya" – was rain dog Tom Waits, who provided a supreme backdrop to the whole trek. PV found himself eulogized on 'Cemetery Polka' and was promptly rechristened Uncle Verner, while 'Transmetropolitan' was shot with 'Singapore' to favour a live charge of "heave away" over the customary yells.

After three days in Holland, half the band took up full time residence at the back of the bus. While Terry, Jem, James and Philip alternated on guitars and banjos, Andrew would be hitting tables, windows and beer cans by way of accompaniment. "One of the things that I've always really liked about the band," says Andrew, "is that it's genuinely about making music in a very realistic and unpretentious way. You can be banging your spoon against a teacup and somebody else might be whistling; it's that simple. And that relates to the majority of music that I like, which is usually played on pretty simple instruments. It can become sophisticated but the area where it begins is an area where anything goes."

At the end of the first week, The Pogues played a one-off French date at Forum des Halles in Paris. During the show, Andrew managed to split the

forefinger of his left hand. Passing the cut off as a hazard of drumming, he did his best to ignore it. But, on reaching Germany, the wound was so badly infected that a doctor warned if he didn't rest his hand for a couple of days the rigid digit might have to be amputated.

Consequently Darryl – freed from driving chores by their increasingly wayward busman, Bill – played drums in Munich. "That was my favourite tour," he remembers. "It was the first time that I didn't have to drive so I was able to get drunk and enjoy myself, as well as doing my job. And basically my most enjoyable time with The Pogues is getting to play with them; nothing can touch that." However, Darryl just didn't have the body weight to match Ranken's whack and Elvis Costello, never far from Cait's side, manned the Pogue sticks on their next night in Freiburg.

The following day they made the short journey across the Swiss border to spend Halloween in Zurich. Beneath the seasonal red luminations of the Röte Fabrik, where Andrew was making a single-handed comeback, the Swiss punks went mental as anything: throwing cans, climbing on stage, and damning to hell the-chocolate-box-and-Heidi-ribbons myth. The band were rejoined by Frank Murray, fresh from England and eager to celebrate the birth of his son, Aran. By 2.30 am, the entourage had settled into their Seegarten Hotel for the long and top heavy task of wetting the Pogueen's head.

Some hours later the bus that swallowed Sergio Leone was heading northward for Frankfurt. As the night's casualties slumped into sleep, the other rain dogs played on. "I think we discovered how musical we potentially were," opines Philip. "It was still at a time when people regarded us as this cute little punk band who play Irish music. And that tour was the turning point where we realized that we weren't going to be continuing to do albums like 'Rum, Sodomy And The Lash' and 'Red Roses For Me', and that it was going to be quite a major leap from them."

Meanwhile, Shane had adopted a daily habit of reading Turkish newspapers. They were, he shrugged, the closest he would come to Greece. Tired of touring, MacGowan's mind was firmly fixed on the middle of the month and the first flight back to London. A few days later, fate served him a helping hand.

Arriving in the Swedish canal city of Malmo, it became clear that Shane's worsening cold was more than a heavy chill. And, three hours before The Pogues were due on stage, a doctor diagnosed pneumonia. As their singer was rushed off to hospital, the rest of the band decided it was too late to cancel the show. The vocals were subsequently shared between Elvis Costello, Spider, Terry and Philip but, before they went on, a steward explained the line-up change to the 600-strong crowd, and told them that ticket refunds were available. Five Swedes headed for the nearest door.

"That was probably the worst gig we've ever done," says Spider. "There's no point in trying to play it straight without Shane 'cos he's obviously such a crucial part of The Pogues. We all got arseholed drunk before we went on, because that's the kind of a night it had turned into, and it was a complete shambles. But at the time it was a real laugh and I think the crowd thought so too."

Afterwards, the band hid from public view in their dressing room, where Frank Murray was feeling less than happy about their abysmal performance and the cancelled schedule. The jaded party was homeward bound.

Having whistled past the graveyard, Shane says, "It was touch and go. When the hospital started treating me they shoved paracetamol up my bum. That felt a bit strange, but some of the nurses were nice." Back home, he was restored to relative health and allowed a couple of precious free weeks.

Towards the end of November, The Pogues had another attempt at the Christmas single for release in January! It was a MacGowan and Finer ballad cum waltz entitled 'A Fairytale Of New York', coupled with an unlikely cover of The Lovin' Spoonful's 'Do You Believe In Magic?' But the former proved exceedingly difficult to record.

"It was a great song," says Paul Scully, "but it never fell together. Shane was less than one hundred per cent happy with the lyrics and kept trying to rewrite them. He wanted strings on it too, which didn't really turn out the way it should have."

The band had, however, managed to get one of their Yuletide acts together. They decided to issue Pogue Christmas cards and, after acquiring the appropriate apparel, they enlisted the services of lensman Tom Collins to re-live the Nativity scene.

Shot against a backdrop of the New York City skyline, Cait and Shane posed as Mary and Joseph; Philip, James and Jem as the Three Wise Men, Spider, Terry, Frank, Paul and Darryl as shepherd allsorts and, as was often the case on such occasions, Andrew Pogue was AWOL.

Brilliant as the photographs were, though, the session had certainly posed its problems. Bethlehem hay was all very authentic but, with more than half a dozen chain smoking Pogues around, Tom Collins had lived in fear that someone would unwittingly set his studio alight.

By the time the cards were ready to post, a 21-date tour of England, Scotland and Ireland was lined up for December. But before taking to the road, Frank Murray called up his former Specials sparring-partner and born Pogue, Dave Jordan, and invited him to take charge of sound monitors.

Dave Jordan moved to London from his home town of Barrow-in-Furness, in 1972, and his varied background included a stint as Island Records' van driver and recording engineer for The Rolling Stones.

In 1979 he worked alongside Elvis Costello on The Specials first LP, and his instinctive under-

The magnificently moody Dave Jordan

standing led to a full-time job with the band and a lasting friendship with their tour manager, Frank Murray.

When The Specials split in the summer of 1981, Jordan took off with Terry Hall, Neville Staples and Lynval Golding, who emerged in October as The Fun Boy Three. He produced their hit single 'The Lunatics (Have Taken Over The Asylum)' and 'The Fun Boy Three' LP but, the following year, Jordan was sacked. "They got fed up of waiting three hours for me to start a session," he quips.

After going on to work with a number of foreign acts, including the Japanese band Sandii And The Sunsetz, he took a sabbatical year in Barrow. He re-emerged in 1984, producing for several artists including Frank Murray's charge Kirsty MacColl.

The Christmas tour opened on December 3 in Sheffield, with a set honed to Pogue perfection.

Ambling on to the familiar strains of 'Paddy Garcia', they seared straight into the manic 'Sick Bed' not letting up till a soulful three-song spell of 'The Old Main Drag', 'A Pair Of Brown Eyes' and 'Dirty Old Town'. Then back to the breakneck with a furious 30-minute mix of instrumentals and old favourites; Cait briefly pausing for a seasonal salute to the Jesus And Mary Chain. By the time they got to the encore and 'Waltzing Matilda', the crowd were united in a singular, full-throated mass. There wasn't a sound in the country to touch them.

And visually, they were more electrifying than ever. The focus, which had once been on Shane and his left-hand cohorts Spider and Cait, was now panoramic. During the Shaneless instrumentals, Philip assumed the role of cheer-leader, while James played fag inhaling dynamo against the distinguished presence of Terry Woods. "I remember a review saying that The Pogues never look at one another," says James, "and for a long time that was the case, but now I love looking round. When Cait makes a mistake on her bass it's really funny to look across and see her looking sheepish about it."

Continuing through Hanley and Liverpool, their trail was marked with the glint of rising status: a luxury tour bus. However, the vehicle belonged not to The Pogues but to their super-fluous support act. They found themselves pack-ed, ever tighter, into a battered Transit.

The tour, and indeed the whole year, reached a climax on December 8, when they sold out the Hammersmith Odeon. "That was the highpoint in lots of ways," comments Paul Scully. "We suddenly realized that we could play London and sell-out a 4,500-seated place with very little posters or hype."

The gig itself was unforgettable. Tommy Keane and Henry Benagh joined in on 'Dirty Old Town' (dedicated to Kirsty "whose dad wrote it") while Elvis Costello appeared for 'The Wild Rover'. Throughout, Shane howled his heart

empty – and the house down.

"That was our most significant gig," says James, "and it was also very important for Frank. I had the feeling that people had written him off, saying that he would never be the manager of a decent group. So it was like him sticking two fingers up at those who said he couldn't do it. I don't go for people getting really cocky about doing anything, but that night was a bit of a triumph for Frank – and it was for us."

They wrapped up the two-week tour by donning kilts in Glasgow's Barrowland Ballroom. It was Spider's 27th birthday. "I can't really say anything about Barrowlands," he says, "'cos I've said it so many times before that I'm probably boring people shitless."

Barrowlands managed to reciprocate the Stacy enthusiasm and among the throng was Nick Stewart. "I don't think The Pogues realize how good or important they are," he says. "It's not just Irish music jazzed up – they're on a different plain. The only person that I can compare them with is Tom Waits."

Simultaneously, Christmas accolades came via *Melody Maker*, who named Shane MacGowan as their Chap Of The Year and 'Rum, Sodomy And The Lash' as second best LP. *NME*, for all their hyperbole, were more effacive: voting 'A Pair Of Brown Eyes' ninth in the singles, and 'Rum' at 18. Meanwhile, Pogues' publicist Philip Hall, was named Press Officer Of The Year for his part in the 'Rum, Sodomy And The Lash' party.

In nine months, Frank Murray had extended The Pogues from a family of eight to 13. Former Rats man, PV was happy to accept a retainer. "Once you start working with a band like The Pogues, it's really difficult to leave," he says. "They're just really genuine people with none of the big rock star bullshit. Everyone is equal, and that's a very rare attitude these days."

It was the same for DJ (Dave Jordan). "When people from earth go to the moon they've got to wear a spacesuit to survive," he smiles. "And for me just surviving on a normal day-to-day basis is difficult, but The Pogues is the ideal environment. It's comfortable, I can function on every level. The people involved are concerned about your welfare but if you want to get fucked up occasionally there's no moralizing, and they're great people; they're good friends."

By Boxing Day, The Pogues were heading out again – for a nationwide tour of Ireland. Cait thought that their flight was the following day and, consequently, it was Darryl who played bass at Waterford's Bridge Hotel. Cait – whose vocals had earned them one of four places in Peel's Festive 50

– arrived in time for Tralee, parading a brand new hairdo and, more subtly, a diamond and emerald ring.

The next two nights revolved around Dublin's SFX and the sanctimonious spa of Bloom's Hotel. And although their actual performances proved disappointing, it made little difference to the defrosting hordes who'd paid £6.50 to see them. These included archpogue Sean Conboy and his friend Mo Brennan, who had caught a ferry in time for their second show, and then hitched through freezing fog in a thwarted attempt to see in 1986 at Belfast's Ulster Hall.

This time round, the band were unperturbed by the critics. The Pogues were simply The Pogues and Ireland, like everywhere else, could love it or shove it.

"We play a certain amount of Irish music," says Terry Woods, "but it isn't designed to be an Irish band. What's important is that people are seeing and getting a sense of fun from the band, and that's one of the reasons why we're attracting such a good audience."

The crack continued through New Year's Day in Dundalk, then it was westward to Mayo and The Beaten Path Ballroom in Claremorris. The entourage included a support duo of Elvis Costello and Ron Kavana, whose singularly Irish blend of r 'n' b had already made him a semi-legend on London's pub circuit. And it was Kavana who labelled Claremorris as the night of the psychoceili. "Claremorris was wonderful," enthuses Philip. "One of the best gigs we've done."

But, by this stage, Frank Murray had returned to London to be at the bedside of his long-time friend, Philip Lynott, who collapsed from kidney and liver failure on Christmas Day. Lynott never regained full consciousness and died on January 4. The Pogues' show at Galway's Leisureland was consequently a night of mourning rather than the 21st birthday celebration for Cait it should have been.

Nevertheless, the tour ended up on a regal note

for Shane when the band played in his heartland of Puckaun, Tipperary. Kennedy's Bar was the scene of wild celebration as he was joined on vocals by a host of glass-in-hand relatives and friends, precariously poised and eagerly awaiting a familiar song.

After a memorable fortnight, The Pogues turned their thoughts to America. "It's always been a dream world to me," says Shane. "Kennedy was a huge hero in my family, because he was Irish American and the first Catholic President of the United States. The late fifties early sixties was a great period of hope for everybody in the Western world and America represented that. And then, bang! The Vietnam war and John Kennedy, Robert Kennedy, Martin Luther King and Malcolm X, all assassinated. In one decade it went from a dream period of affluence and everybody looking to America to the shit heap that everything is now. But, I want to go there. I'm fascinated by all the different cultures: the Irish, the Italians, the Puerto Ricans, the Japs, they're all American but they still have their own cultures. I'm obsessed with it for loads of reasons."

The band's long-anticipated trip was finally arranged for February.

a fairytale of new york

It was a long way from Tipperary to here, and back to Harlesden it seemed even further. But The Pogues had aroused interest in France and, on January 16, TV producer Antoin Des Caunes braved the Hampstead divide to capture them at The Mean Fiddler.

The night was a riot: Saint Patrick came early as a sea of green flooded beyond the rafters and the band blazed holy mayhem in the place they loved so well. The highlights formed the basis of a half-hour documentary which traced their roots from Ireland to the pubs of Cricklewood, King's Cross and Camden Town. It featured Shane in his natural habitat of the Devonshire Arms, Elvis Costello at the mixing desk and video clips from 'A Pair Of Brown Eyes' and 'Waxies Dargle'.

The Pogues spent the next two weeks in the studio. They had eventually abandoned 'Fairytale Of New York' and opted instead for an EP. "In a sense we felt that the time was right to do an album," says Philip, "but 'Rum, Sodomy And The Lash' had only just come out. So rather than doing a single we decided to show four different sides to the group."

The EP, titled 'Poguetry In Motion', began with 'London Girl' an uptempo breeze around the capital rich in accordion and their most commercial sound to date. 'The Body Of An American' is a return to traditional concerns: the love of home, the loss of home and the endless quest for roots.

With Spider Stacy in the foreground it verves along as only an Irish wake could; Tommy Keane piping the plaintive touch.

The final mix was 'Planxty Noel Hill', an instrumental from the hand of Jem Finer, and a manic tribute to the pedantic Hill who had taken such exception to the non-purist Pogues on B P Fallon's radio show. "Noel Hill is generally a nice man," says Terry Woods diplomatically, "but he missed the point completely, so we thought we'd dedicate something to him."

'Poguetry In Motion' was recorded at Elephant Studios and produced, once again, by Elvis Costello. Since Christmas, the relationship between Declan Patrick Aloysius MacManus and Caitlin O'Riordan had gone conspicuously public. O'Riordan appeared on the songwriting credits for Costello's comeback LP, 'King Of America', and featured on the video for 'Don't Let Me Be Misunderstood'.

Less prosperous, however, was the working

relationship between Costello and the rest of The Pogues. During 'Poguetry In Motion' it became clear that Costello's views were irredeemably out of synch with the band's and Dave Jordan ended up producing the final version of 'A Rainy Night In Soho'. Enhanced by horns and full strings, it's a heart-rending ballad that captures all the romance and ghost-grey allure of Soho. 'I took shelter from a shower and I stepped into your arms/ On a rainy night in Soho the wind was whistling all its charms/ Sometimes I wake up in the morning/ the Ginger Lady by my bed/ covered in a cloak of silence/ I hear you talking in my head/ I'm not singing for the future/ I'm not dreaming of the past/ I'm not talking of the first times/ I never think about the last . . .'   Shane considered it their finest recording ever. "It's a very personal song," he says, "and so was 'A Pair Of Brown Eyes', but 'Rainy Night In Soho' was more successful. It's the closest that we've ever got to the way that I thought a song should sound."

The Pogues had every intention of making a video for 'Poguetry In Motion', and Neil Jordan was suggested as a possible director. And although it never materialized, they are the only band that Jordan – the man behind *Angel*, *Company Of Wolves* and, at the time, working on *Mona Lisa* – admits to listening to. "I like The Pogues a lot," he says. "They remind me of Luke Kelly who was a very great Irish singer."

Pressed for time, the band had to abandon the idea of a video, and turn their attention to Alex Cox's Sid Vicious and Nancy Spungeon movie, *Love Kills*. Cox screened a roughcut of the terminal romance and invited them to contribute some music to the soundtrack. After experimenting with various instruments, they came up with the atmospheric 'Junk Theme': an instrumental written by Finer, arranged by himself, Chevron and Fearnley and produced by Dave Jordan.

"It was after hearing 'Rain Dogs' in Germany that we started talking about different sounds," says James. "I discovered that if you get a man-

dolin on your knees, dampen two of the strings and hit it with teaspoons you get a really individual noise. We used that on 'Junk', which starts off pretty straightforwardly then goes off into loads of things. There's violin, banjo, accordion, mandolin, bass, drums, guitar, auto-harp; we just piled everything on."

Elephant became the centre of an unlikely dirge as Jem and Spider taught themselves saxophone, and Shane turned up with a trumpet. The band were still working on the film music when the EP hit the shops and it was time, at last, for their self-styled Poguetry Kills Tour.

Mid-day in late February saw them bound for New York via Air India. Not a comfortable thought as they flew 33,000 feet over the west coast of Ireland, and less soothing still when it became crystal clear that the airline wasn't prepared for wholesale consumption from the cocktail cabinet. Frank Murray sighed, May God preserve Aer Lingus.

Several hours later they found themselves in the more salubrious setting of the Iroquois Hotel, a rough and ready apartment block, standing on West 44th Street, and favoured by Bohemians of every persuasion.

Although 'Red Roses' and 'Rum' were only available on import, The Pogues caused an immediate stir. Both MTV and college radio had picked up on 'A Pair Of Brown Eyes' and, as a preliminary to their visit, Murray secured the services of a reputed PR agency. Consequently, the band spent the first two days in their publicist's cramped office doing an unending stream of interviews.

By the night of their opening show, on February 28, even the prestigious dailies were requesting freebies. "*The New York Times* never came here in their life!" exclaimed the manager of the highly celebrated World, as he watched The Pogues sell out at a cool 15 bucks a head. What's more, the reaction was far from blasé: the star-spangled crowd jigged and yelled like the best of them.

"The World was a real highlight," enthuses Terry Woods. "New York is a very sophisticated audience, because it gets everything that's going. You could easily die a death there, but we were lucky enough to be successful."

The Pogues had previously been described as Clancy Brothers with earrings, and among the many revellers that night was mega movie-lust Matt Dillon. "Hey, I was raised on that shit," he told the band. "You guys, I really dig your shit."

"He came back to the dressing room after the show and started singing Clancy Brothers' songs to us," remembers Philip. "He knew more about The Clancy Brothers than I did!"

New York was certainly living up to expectations and had already done wonders for their Al 'hey, fuck you, muthafucka' Pacino impressions. "Going to New York was the best thing that I've done in this band," asserts Spider. "It's completely fuckin' mad."

The first day of March saw the World-worn party pacing the Iroquois in a vain wait for their bass player. But the bright light city had proved too much: Caitlin had gone home, again.

After a futile attempt to intercept her at JFK Airport, The Pogues handed the bass to ever-ready Darryl, and veered south on the four-hour route to Washington, DC. Their driver was Bill Rahmy, a momentous figure from Springfield, Massachusetts, who not only served Skeeter Davis but also played a convincing courier.

Their destination was the downtown haunt of the hip and happening: the 930 Club on Ford Street. And, despite the lack of Cait, the response couldn't have been better. Washington adored them.

The next day involved a 40 mile backtrack, through Maryland to Baltimore. A vibrant port, long since revered in ballad form by Glaser/ Howard's supreme 'Streets Of Baltimore', The Pogues were directed to the less than spacious, but appropriately named, Eight By Ten Club.

Far from suffering under Maryland's restricted licensing laws, the entourage enjoyed excessive generosity and unlimited free beer. It was hardly surprising that, come midnight, Shane had to be physically placed on stage and, after a few anxious moments trying to locate the mike, he launched himself into 'Streams Of Whiskey'. The band were playing 'Sick Bed'. . .

By the end of the show, the devil couldn't have defined debauched better: Shane so earnestly pursued pleasure that he had the misfortune to overtake it. He passed out in a corner.

Monday morning sent them northward to New York. The wind at their backs, as 'Poguetry In Motion' resounded from the radio. "I was very impressed by the fact that they'd obviously heard us quite a lot," says Jem. "Everywhere we went there seemed to be poxy little shops with 'Poguetry In Motion' in the window, and college radio was playing it all the time; which was unbelievable for somewhere we'd never actually been to before. But it sounded entirely right: it's music that fits in with any old bollocks you want to put on the radio. All sorts of people like it, not just those with particular haircuts. I know people up to the age of 90 who think it's really good, which is great. I reckon we can make records that anyone of any age would buy, and in 50 years time will still be really good songs."

Back in the metropolis they played a press show at the ultra-hip Limelight Club. Among the attendants were the former New York Doll David Johansen, and movie stars David Keith, Molly Ringwald and lifetime convert Matt Dillon. The five-song set seemed all too brief and the audience refused to let the band off stage. Booing, stamping feet and lighting matches eventually brought two encores.

Later, the delighted management unwisely granted The Pogues free licence to the Limelight VIP Lounge, where Spider managed to complicate his life by falling irretrievably in love with a stunning singer named Cheyne.

The following day Cait was back, tipping up in time for their Maxwell's date in nearby Hoboken. O'Riordan's sudden departure was nothing more than a smashed memory, best explained by American generosity. "Whatever their motives might be," she says, "they give you free drink as soon as you want it, for as long as you're conscious and even afterwards sometimes. I was just full of vodka and consequently went extremely psychotic for a few days, but I sobered up. Once I was away from the free drink and the fawning, I was fine."

While Cait retrieved her bass Darryl resumed his driving duties, transporting the gear from New York to the Massachusetts college town of Northampton. The band travelled, per usual, with Bill who was particularly enthused as they drove towards his beloved Springfield Valley. "One thing that I really like about working with these guys," he says, "is that they aren't hardened cowboys. The highways are new to them so it's good fun showing them around. They've really made me appreciate America."

The next day they drove 90 miles to Boston where, on arriving at Spit/DV8 (formerly the Boston Tea Party), The Pogues were hit by an air of expectation, normally reserved for London, Glasgow or Dublin. "There are certain places that seem to adopt us," articulates Philip. "You can feel it almost as soon as you get there."

The crowd were barely contained as the overzealous leapt on and off stage and one, with admirable abandon, even dangled from the rigging. The rest of the hall chanted verses and choruses alike, giving 'The Wild Rover' its definitive treatment and generating a glow that the house lights couldn't hope to dim.

"The reaction was quite amazing," stated hardened trouper PV. "The whole American attitude is, 'You're starting off in the clubs so therefore we shouldn't like you' and, of all the bands I've worked with, I've never seen anyone get a response like that. I just wish more people could have witnessed it."

After the show, the dressing room was stormed by fans: several bearing Nips and Radiators singles that even Shane and Philip weren't aware of. Later, they discovered that their audience had included the sons of the late Presidents John and Bobby Kennedy. Midway through an election campaign, Joseph Kennedy and his cousin John Kennedy Jnr had been discussing a fund-raising event in the Metro Club when they inquired who was playing next door. On hearing that it was The Pogues they went to Spit/DV8 and stayed for the whole set.

The non-stop trail continued to Rhode Island and the beautiful city of Providence, where they headlined a four-band bill at Lupo's Heartbreak Hotel. And finally, on March 8, The Pogues returned to New York for a farewell show at Chelsea's hyped-out Danceteria. "The way the tour worked out was great," says James. "We kept coming back to New York so there was press, radio interviews and reviews. Each time there was a bit more of a buzz, and by the third time it seemed like the whole bloody place was crying out for us."

Back in London, they had reached 28 in the charts with 'Poguetry In Motion'. 'London Girl' had finally overcome Radio 1's playlist, while 'A Rainy Night In Soho' was a constant sound on RTE. Simultaneously, they won a series of accolades in the *NME* Readers' Poll including Best Live Act. By way of cruel illustration they were crammed into a hired van and, still jetlagged senseless, packed off to Newcastle and Leeds.

Two days later The Pogues toasted Saint Patrick at the Hammersmith Palais. By now, their annual celebration was imbued with a religious significance of its own. The show had sold out in February, the pubs had filled by noon and early evening Hammersmith heaved with green as young Irish, old Irish and sheer wishful-thinking Irish, headed for the Palais.

While Terry Woods and Philip Chevron guested on the Janice Long Show, the others were besieged by press. Tetchy from articulating the case, Shane told *The Observer*: "It's hard for us to take in words with more than eight letters. We don't try to be serious or philosophical. Then we'd be boring like all the others." Sidestepping the spotlight he tried, instead, to revive his wilting shamrock. MacGowan wasn't, as Declan Lynch observed in *Hot Press*, "revealing the secret of his talent to anyone, and only a fool would ask."

By 8.00 pm the Palais was the scene of rapidly accelerating chaos. Downstairs, a euphoric army of headers and hipsters converged; on stage, Ron Kavana bravely battled with a solo acoustic set; backstage, the dressing room overflowed with family and friends. And outside, a ticketless queue stretched longer than the Liffey.

Eventually, The Pogues took the stage and played possessed. Fuelled by the excess of the occasion, their set was wilder than ever and the crowd responded in kind, the opening numbers barely audible as the noise rose to a manic mixture of Croke Park, the Stretford End and Parkhead. "I suppose we come across a bit like a football team," says Philip. "Because we don't look like Duran Duran or wear Anthony Price suits or John Paul Gaultier underpants, we look pretty much like the male members of our audience. Consequently we are – and especially Shane – regarded by other males as ordinary blokes that you could meet in the pub and have a laugh and a drink with."

The warmest cheer however, was saved for Cait who raised a smiling slainte and dedicated 'I'm A Man You Don't Meet Every Day' to "everyone who likes a drink."

Fourteen hours later they returned to Hammersmith for a tamer, but technically improved, second show. Meanwhile, a series of French festivals and TV shows had been lined up for the following week so, the next day, it was back to the studio in a rushed attempt to finish their contribution to *Love Kills*.

On this occasion they took to Lansdowne House in Notting Hill, to remix 'Junk' and record 'A Needle For Paddy Garcia', an instrumental, detailing the further adventures of Jem Finer's fictitious hero.

Afterwards they attempted 'Hot Dogs With Everything', a less than cultured trip around Soho. "I can't sing that!" screeched Spider on reading Shane's scrawled lyrics. Eventually he did, and Stacy's Chainsaw schooling had never served him better. "It was a good laugh," he smiles. "I'm not keen on recording because, apart from everything else, I'm always the last one to do anything, so I just have to sit around the studio; but I really enjoyed doing 'Hot Dogs'."

The following night, having completed their studio work, Spider and Shane went to a nearby restaurant with Alex Cox who was now planning a rock 'n' roll documentary to be filmed in Nicaragua during August and starring The Pogues and Joe Strummer. Afterwards they headed home but, as Shane was about to get into a car in Westbourne Grove, he was hit by a taxi cab. He was thrown into the air, flung 15 yards down the road and left unconscious on the pavement. "For a split second I thought he was dead," says Spider. "I never want to experience anything like that again."

And neither did Shane. He was rushed to hospital where he was found to have multiple injuries including a fractured arm, facial wounds requiring stitches and severe damage to ligaments in his leg. Following an operation over the weekend, MacGowan's arm and leg were put in cast. And, although he discharged himself five days later, he was trapped in plaster for the next four weeks.

Consequently The Pogues had to cancel not only their heavy French schedule, but also an ensuing tour of Germany. "I was still in Dublin," says Paul Scully, "when Frank rang and said, 'We're not going to Paris, we're off to Helsinki.' He made a joke; he's a terrible man. There's a lot of catalysts in this band, and it seems that whenever we've been working really hard and everyone

is mentally and physically at breaking point, something happens and everyone gets a rest. Unfortunately, there's a price to pay and Shane has had to bear the brunt of it both times."

Ill-starred as Shane's health seemed to be, it was certainly conducive to creativity. He acquired a Casio keyboard and spent the next month working out a series of new songs. These included a manic Arabic/Irish number which he christened 'Turkish Song Of The Damned'. The title had arisen in Berlin, when a fan had mentioned the B-side of a Damned single. "Did you ever, you know, hear the 'Turkish Song' of The Damned?" the German had asked. "Aaaaghh! Fuck! What did he say?" shrieked Shane, "The Turkish Song Of The Damned!" The line was a gift, but the resulting song contained some of his most spectral imagery to date: 'I come old friend from hell tonight, across the rotting sea/ Not the nails on the cross nor the blood of Christ, can bring you help this eve . . .''

"Basically it's an historical number," says Shane, "that's more or less like 'Down In The Ground Where The Dead Men Go' or 'Sea Shanty'. It's a ghost story about a bloke who got off a ship and the rest of them went down. It doesn't specify what he did, but it was his fault. It's about being possessed but it's also a bit of a laugh."

To emphasise his increasing power as a wordsmith, Liam Clancy and Tommy Makem asked MacGowan to write a song for them. The result was a very sentimental ballad, lovingly titled 'The Broad Majestic Shannon'. "I'm a sentimental person," he admits, "so I just wrote a song about Tipperary when I was a kid. It's about meeting people, who are around the same age as you that you knew then and there and meeting them now in London, and the way that all the stuff that we loved when we were kids has gone. It's basically just about the good old days and they're gone, and we've got to accept it; I've got to accept it."

Throughout the April evenings, Shane and DJ could invariably be found in Camden's core of cordiality, The Devonshire, where they conceived another outlet know as Shit. It was to be an occasional and less than serious band featuring Mo O'Hagan, Bryan Scully and the incorrigible Paul Ronan.

Shit subsequently made their first appearance, on May 3, at the Town And Country Club in Kentish Town. Having promised toilet tunes for all, they threw up a torrent of forgotten classics including The Nips' 'King Of The Bop'. Spider Stacy, always ready for an impromptu spot, grabbed a spare mike and hurled abuse at anyone gullible enough to listen.

A week later Jem and James made a début of a different kind. Transporting their instruments in a supermarket trolley, they headed for the unlikely venue of Thomas Coram's Nursery School, where they played to a roomful of Ella Finer's classmates.

Due to indoor regulations dancing was strictly prohibited, but a raucous rendition of 'Baa Baa Black Sheep' proved too much and the under fives finally took to the floor during 'Dingle Regatta'. Luckily, by this time, it had stopped raining and a distraught teacher was able to redirect the gathering to the infinitely more suitable playground. And, although the show never regained its early momentum, the offshoot Pogues scored a mass hit and were urged to return.

In the interim, The Pogues proper had completed a final track for *Sid 'n' Nancy: Love Kills*. 'Haunted' is a clangorous pop ballad written by MacGowan, sung by O'Riordan and produced by Craig Leon. The final cut was, however, one that nobody was entirely happy with. "It all went wrong in the mix as far as I'm concerned," says Philip. "We wanted to remix it but there wasn't a chance. On the rough mixes it sounded pretty well like us, there was enough individuality and guts to make it sound like a Pogues record. But it sounds a little bit too American; a little bit too FM. We just didn't have as much control over it as we should have had."

The Pogues returned to the boards in Dublin. Under a collective banner of Self-Aid they appeared alongside U2, The Chieftains, Van Morrison, The Boomtown Rats, Christy Moore and Elvis Costello at the Royal Dublin Showground. Inspired by the spirit of Live Aid, Self-Aid was dedicated to the nation's unemployed and billed as the ultimate exhibition of Irish rock.

Although only 30,000 could be squeezed into the stadium, the rest of the country received round the clock coverage from RTE. The majority of the crowd were young fans and, for one day at least, everybody seemed refreshingly indifferent to the great purist versus rogue debate.

Each act was limited to 15 minutes and, early in the afternoon, The Pogues made the most of theirs. No one was disappointed as they sped through 'Sick Bed' and 'The Body Of An American' before uniting the whole of Dublin under the heartfelt strains of 'Dirty Old Town'.

Backstage, The Chieftains' unsurpassable piper Paddy Maloney handed his instrument to Shane and invited him to have a go. MacGowan immediately turned to Spider, saying: "He's the whistle player not me." Stacy, oblivious to the stature of his audience, proceeded to play. "It wasn't until afterwards that I found out who he was," he says. "Otherwise I'd never have attempted it."

During the evening, Elvis Costello sang Little Willie John's 'Leave My Kitten Alone' for "Cait, my kitten from Clare", who ended the weekend with a gold wedding band and the title of Mrs Costello.

The night closed with an emotional tribute to the late Philip Lynott. Thin Lizzy's Gary Moore and Scott Gorham led the way with 'Don't Believe A Word', before being joined by Bob Geldof for 'The Cowboy Song', and finally by most of the Self-Aid cast in a thronged chorus of 'Whiskey In The Jar'. "That was the part that really got to you," says Spider.

Two weeks later, The Pogues returned to the road for a full-scale assault on France, punctuated with a regrettable five-day visit to Finland. This time the entourage included Davey and Stephen Wiseman, a pair of busking brothers who hailed from Lugton, near Kilmarnock, and were known as the Nyah Fearties. They came to the band's attention via Nick Stewart from Shotts who, on hearing a demo, considered The Fearties the third best band in the world; overshadowed only by The Velvet Underground and The Pogues themselves. Having played to Spider and Philip on a cold January night outside The Devonshire, The Fearties persuaded Frank Murray to give them a support slot, first, at Hammersmith Palais and, now, eight dates in France.

They reached Paris on May 30, just in time for a Friday session at the Right Bank's over-extolled nightspot Les Bains Douche. Not long enough afterwards, they faced a hazy-eyed afternoon and made their way to the north west of the city for a massive Anti-Apartheid Benefit. It was an all-day event, staged on the open park of the Porte de Pantin and organized, among others, by ex-Specials star and leading Artist Against Apartheid, Jerry Dammers.

As soon as they arrived, The Pogues were struck by an unprecedented flash of cameras and press. Microphones probed for attention while shutters shifted into motor-drive for a 20-minute rattle, resembling nothing so much as a scene from Philip Kaufman's *The Right Stuff*. The main subject of attention was Shane who, with supreme nonchalance, barely blinked throughout the wrangle.

Meanwhile, the ever-enterprising Fearties found a venue of their own, temporarily squeezing out the CND slogans and hot dog vendors to play a short, side-stall set.

Dusk was falling when The Pogues finally took the stage, and the cameras rolled again. "I've been sent 90 miles to see this band," hissed a reporter from Reims as he jostled for the front. "I've heard they send the English wild, but they won't do that here, the French always dance like they're listening to Tchaikovsky."

Shane with Paddy Moloney at Self Aid, May 1986

He couldn't have been more wrong. From the first note of 'Sick Bed', the crowd were as manic as the flash bulbs. A huge video screen projected the charge to the back of the field, and the ceili-flavour of 'Wild Cats' and 'Sally MacLennane' sent the entire place into a full-scale reel.

The performance itself was, by Pogue standards, disturbingly mediocre; rarely had they sounded so jaded. Playing a well-worn set might be necessary, but it was also increasingly frustrating. "We've already established a formula," says Andrew, "so, in a way, we could just be The Pogues and carry on playing gigs. But we want to develop and try as many different things as possible. And although I think we'll always have our own sound, there's loads of different influences that we're starting to incorporate: such as soul, jazz and blues; which I think will come out more and more."

Their next date took them south to Marseille's Theatre du Moulin, a velveteen venue decorated exclusively in red, but whose plush seats and rich decor seemed alarmingly at odds with The Pogues, and their protégés.

Let loose with acoustic guitars, vociferous voices and a shopping trolley for a percussion section, The Fearties raucous blend of spaghetti-western and hobo blues sent the crowd rabid, and by the time The Pogues appeared, the red walls couldn't have reverberated louder. 'Waltzing Matilda' certainly inspired the strangest effect when, amid collective screams, a frenzied woman clambered on stage and played Gypsy Rose Lee to gog-eyed starletch Spider Stacy.

The next three nights, in Toulouse, Bordeaux and Orleans, saw a further scramble of howls, shrieks and uncontrolled delight. "I think the humanity of the band comes across, and people pick up on the spirit of that," says Philip. "It's something that a group like The Band seemed to have and if you look at 'The Last Waltz' you can see the sort of family atmosphere that they had.

OK, they ended up completely screwed up because they'd been on the road too long, but there was a comradeship that is very important."

After a five-day stint of summer festivals in Finland, they hit Lyon. Spider, now in the throes of glandular fever, felt less than his live-wire self, but couldn't resist the sound of Kilmarnock soul. He rushed on to The Fearties' set, singing 'Drunken Sailor', impulsively followed by Mad Guitar Chevron and crazed drummers, Ranken and Scully, who ran to the back, battering everything they could lay their hands on.

The tour reached its zenith at Maison de la Mutalite in Paris, where The Pogues were swamped by an insatiable press and a glowing record company. The latter voiced its appreciation with a massive cake baked in the shape of an anchor; later presented (without ceremony) to someone misguided enough to steal Jem Finer's beer.

Within 10 days, The Pogues were to embark on a three-week tour of north America but, back home, their live work continued. June 17 saw a birthday appearance on *Whistle Test* and a dramatic recovery in Philip Chevron who had, throughout the French trip, been racked by severe depression. "I really did have some nightmarish times," he says. "I became quite irrational and uncontrollable. There wouldn't be any particular thing that would spark it off; that was the frightening thing. But in situations like that, to use an old cliché, you know who your friends are, and it was well and truly driven home to me that – with the exception of my family and three or four other people who really matter – my friends are in this group."

Their *Whistle Test* set included 'The Body Of An American', 'Dirty Old Town', and 'Streams Of Whiskey' – sounding as inspired as when it was written nearly half a decade before. "It sums up the devil-may-care, romantic side of our attitude," says Shane. "Well it sums up part of it. The fact that we don't give a shit; but not in a negative way. At the time I wrote it, I believed that drinking a lot of whiskey was a good thing; that it led through one of the doors of perception. And it does. What I don't actually believe any more, is that whiskey is the best way."

The rest of the week took The Pogues to Margate, Nottingham, Glastonbury and Sheffield. This time, rather than reverting to the usual hired van, they travelled by coach; and Murray's extravagance even stretched to a specially drafted tour manager named Joey Cashman, a friend of Philip Chevron's who knew the rest of the band. Once again the party included The Fearties, who not only acted as support but also provided a cameo Pogue show by breakdancing their way through 'Jesse James'.

On June 24, The Pogues flew to Washington, DC, and discovered that, since the experimental tour in February, their profile had shot even higher. Writing in that month's issue of *SPIN*, Glenn O'Brien said: "Although they play Irish traditional music – more or less – this band will blow you away. They're hard. They play with fantastic intensity. Seeing them changes everything."

They were met by Massachusetts Bill, who abandoned courier duties to act as tour manager, and at the wheel was Lyle – a diamond driver from Nashville, Tennessee.

The opening show was a high-spirited affair at the city's Nightclub, which saw Spider sporting a split forehead. He claimed that he had fallen out of bed the previous night and nobody felt disposed to inquire further. The damage was promptly repaired by a self-styled Trauma Technician, who embroidered four stitches in Stacy's skull.

While The Pogues were in Philadelphia, Frank Murray was in New York where, on the eve of their Ritz début, ticket sales were incredibly high. Later, he visited their euphoric publicist who confirmed that the show was sold-out, and gushed, "The Pogues are going to be my U2."

Murray remained stoical until after the gig. But not only did The Pogues attract 1500 to the

prestigious ballroom, they sent them into excelsus. "New York audiences are so blasé," said Frank, suitably impressed. "You have to work really hard to get them going."

The band certainly did their utmost: Spider seized a beer-tray and – without a second's heed on the Trauma Technician – bashed his brains through 'The Battle Of Brisbane', while James and Terry gave 'The Old Main Drag' the full works with accordion versus concertina. "Terry is really good for playing off," says James. "I never believed in this much; it's something that rock journalists write about, you know, Keith Richards and Ron Wood. But on 'The Old Main Drag' and 'Jesse James' we're both playing around the same chords yet Terry makes me play something different. So in a way it's like a competition."

After the show they headed round the corner to Tramps, a popular Irish bar famed for the blues. The drinks flowed freely but, by dawn, Cait's conscience was pricked. "What do you think we get paid for?" she demanded. The majority subsequently returned to the hotel, although several escaped for another round. "The Pogues," quipped Terry, "the only band to take the breathalizer before a gig."

Woods and Murray's post-gig getaways had by now evolved into legend, and it was less than shocking to see them finally turn in at breakfast time. Later that day, the others got even by baptizing Terry 'Tonto' and Frank 'The Lone Ranger'.

Although they easily adjusted from Greenwich Mean to US Eastern, Pogue Time remained a law unto itself. Home or away, their departures were invariably delayed by at least an hour, and the trip to Trenton was no exception. When they eventually left, the party was all but lifeless. One notable exception was Jem who picked up a guitar and learnt a highly stylized version of Prince's 'Kiss'. "Most of the tunes I make up are the result of me trying to work out how to play something else," he says. "My ears are so bad that I just make

loads of mistakes and end up with completely different tunes altogether. It's really handy."

Trenton might be New Jersey's state capital, but from The City Gardens it was strictly a one-horse hole. The hall itself was new and spacious, generously accommodating two bars, a likely magnet for the weekend rednecks.

Cait was quickly surrounded by a large quota of ingratiating fans and, though polite, she had visibly had enough of Trenton. "I love Los Angeles," she says, "and fortunately that was right at the end. That's what got me through all the shit, 'Oh, we're going to be in LA in two weeks; don't leave, don't leave.' I was counting off the days."

After the soundcheck, half the troupe ensconced themselves in Trenton's finest asset: a long bar called Romeo's, cheap and friendly and a perpetual haunt for local cops.

Back at The City Gardens, Mojo Nixon and Skid Roper, support for the whole tour, took the stage. Their offbeat mixture of blues, gospel and de-railed rock'n'roll, was a winner with the studded rhinestone set.

Later, The Pogues' impact was best measured by those willing to forsake a place at the bar in favour of amassing by the stage. When the show was done, the band entertained college radio with a series of over-the-air impressions – Jem as Prince, PV a convincing Ronnie Drew and Spider doing a Highland crossbreed of his own. Hey, these Pogues are really crazy! "One more," urged the reporter, "Just one more!". A second's silence. Then Jem spoke, deadpan: "Get the fuck out of Nicaragua."

After a day-off in New York, it was onward to New Haven. They were joined by Joey Cashman who, on his way to a month's holiday in Providence, caught the band at The Ritz and was subsequently asked to roadie instead.

Toad's Place was close to Yale University, and proved typical of New Haven: a thoroughly American mixture of pool room and dance hall. As soon as the band arrived they launched into a

lengthy series of interviews, and many of the questions inevitably centred on the Irish angle.

"The Irishness is more in the feel now of what we do than what we actually play," says Philip. "It seems to me, though, that we can say until we're blue in the face that a) we're not Irish and b) we don't play Irish music but no one will believe us. I think the Americans will always regard us as an Irish band whatever we do. We could put out an electronic music album and MCA would stick a shamrock on the sleeve! It's not worth getting upset about. All we're trying to get across is that there's more to us than the Irish aspect."

Two nights later they filled Boston's Metro with an atmosphere that was as close as Massachusetts was likely to get to Ireland. Despite serious sound problems, audience and band were one: united in wild abandon, brilliant music and sheer good will. The Pogues returned for four encores and finally disappeared to deafening approval when Cait grabbed the mike and told Boston, "We love you". What they had tonight could never be lost.

Two days later it was time for Canada. During their second night at Quebec City's Summer Festival, The Pogues were faced with an all-seated crowd of 2,000, most of whom would never see 50 again. "It was totally different from the normal audience," remembers Jem. "Ninety five per cent of the people there were very straight and conservative, but they were quite warm and clapped politely. Then about half way through we told them that we didn't mind if they danced, and at the end a lot of them were standing up and cheering and we got quite a few encores. It was a good experience 'cos there was no way you could say that we were playing to a captive audience; we really had to work to get across. It also proved that the music appeals to anyone."

Back in the States, their appearance at the Columbus Music Theatre ended in exploding egos and a wrecked dressing room, an incident not unconnected with the band's early evening con-

sumption of mescal. The rare discovery of miniature bottles meant mescal-soaked worms for everyone, and Shane and Spider rabidly indulged in four worms each.

The remaining dates took them to Detroit, Chicago and Los Angeles. Before appearing at Chicago's Vic, they headed for Briar Street Theatre to watch *Frank's Wild Years*, the stage production written by Tom Waits and his wife Kathleen Brennan. Since Waits was doing two shows that night he was unable to catch The Pogues live, but he joined them on an aftergig bar-hop.

Their jaunt encompassed a late night session around a backbar piano: Cait and Elvis delivered a couple of duets and James played an offbeat tango, but for the most part it was Waits playing and The Pogues singing.

"The Pogues were in town and came to see the play," says Waits. "Then Kathleen went to see their show. She flipped. You have to give them awards for standing up first of all and anything that follows . . . afterwards we all went out to a bar and got up and sang and played all night. Yeah, The Pogues are something else."

The tour closed on July 14 with a sold-out show at the Hollywood Palace. But The Pogues went home on a controversial note. MCA had pulled 'Hot Dogs With Everything' from the *Love Kills* soundtrack, following objections to the 'obscene' lyrics. The record company felt that the 'risqué' song would fall short of United States decency laws, and rather than just taking it off the non-American version of the LP they played safe and removed it altogether.

By this time, the Pogues were less than happy with MCA marketing. Mid-way through the tour, they had learned that the record company's art department were using the cover of 'Poguetry In Motion' to do Shane a favour – they had filled in his teeth. Murray immediately ordered them to stop. "Americans are obsessed with dental hygiene," he says. "They spend more money on

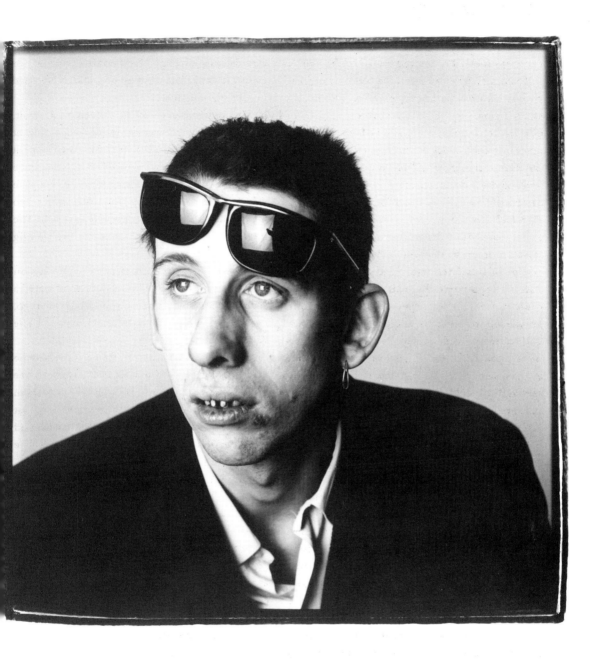

their teeth than they do on their brains."

Murray's anger was further fuelled when he read in a Los Angeles newspaper of "The tawdry release of The Pogues album 'Rum, Sodomy And The Lash' by MCA."

"It's very hard to get American record companies to think," he sighs. "They like formulas: hard rock, soft rock and so on. And someone from MCA had obviously listened to the album in an office – without being aware of our status in Britain and Europe – and just thought, 'What the fuck is this? Take it off!' They also had this Irish band called Cactus World News and they were trying to promote them because they thought they had another U2. We did two tours in America: packed out all the places we played and got very good press, and now I just feel that those tours were a waste of time. There was no reflection in record sales, simply because MCA wasn't trying to sell the record."

Meanwhile in London, Stiff were on the verge of collapse. They had been in serious financial straits for several months, and it was only by outflanking their creditors and transferring their assets to a new company (Stiff Records) that they managed to keep afloat. The long list of creditors did not, however, include either The Pogues or Kirsty MacColl. "That," says Frank, "is because Frank Murray is their manager."

Following the première of *Sid 'n' Nancy* on July 20, Alex Cox was all set for his next project. Financial limitations had forced him to postpone the planned documentary on Nicaragua, so he decided to feature The Pogues and Joe Strummer in a spoof spaghetti-western instead. Titled *The Legend Of Paddy Garcia*, the movie was scripted in three and a half days by Cox and actor Dick Rude,

and was to be shot in Southern Spain during August. The Pogues consequently spent the rest of July in the rehearsal room preparing more film music.

Simultaneously, 'A Pair Of Brown Eyes' was given alternative treatment by American singer/ songwriter Peter Case. He chose MacGowan's song as the final track on his critically acclaimed 'Peter Case' LP. "The bloke hasn't got a clue what he's singing about," sneers Cait. "He's done it 'cos it's a nice melody and he thinks it's cool. But he just doesn't know what he's singing, so it's like a foreign language."

O'Riordan considered their own version of 'Brown Eyes' to be the best song ever recorded. "Shane's got such a brilliant, emotive voice," she says. "If we had a different singer – even if it was someone who could write the same songs – then maybe we wouldn't come across. 'Cos Shane's voice is so bloody emotive that whatever he's singing: sentimental shit, hard shit, his own shit, shit shit – he can really put it over."

On August 2, The Pogues travelled to Birmingham's National Exhibition Centre for the YIVA! Festival, an Oxfam/Artists Against Apartheid benefit for the oppressed of South Africa and Namibia. It was an all-day event featuring eight other acts and a handful of media celebrities. The Pogues were accompanied, as usual, by Elvis Costello who was also to appear in Alex Cox's film. By now, Cait and Elvis were verging on the glossy couple ranks of Bob and Paula and Mick and Jerry. "We're the Sonny and Cher of the eighties," Costello told the tabloids, "and I'm Cher."

During YIVA!, which was to be the band's only English date for four months, Cait momentarily considered the disadvantages of being a Pogue, and said: "The biggest drawback is putting up with these drunken bastards, when they are drunken bastards. Sometimes they're absolutely loveable. They're the Virgin Mary and Pope John Paul all rolled into one at the same time, but sometimes

. . . It was fine when I was as pissed as they were – or even more drunk – but now that I'm a refined, mature young lady, I find it all a bit wearing.

"No," she added, "I love them. I wouldn't be without them."

Sandwiched between Ruby Turner and Feargal Sharkey, The Pogues received YIVA!'s loudest welcome, and a routine stroll through a short set left few disappointed. "Thank God for The Pogues!" cried *Sounds*. "Thank God for The Pogues!" echoed *NME*. No such praise was offered for the redredged King, who had insisted on headlining and were promptly bottled to the back of the stage.

As a prelude to Spain, The Pogues returned to France for a 10-day round of summer festivals. The sites ranged from an outdoor Celtic celebration in Brittany's Lorient to the Roman amphitheatre at Nîmes and a bullring in the southern town of Mont-de-Marsan.

Their next port of call was Almeria, a coastal town on the edge of Spain's Sierra Nevada. Less than 20 miles away stood Mini-Hollywood, the desert setting for *Lawrence Of Arabia* and *The Greatest Story Ever Told* but, more significantly, the Wild West backdrop to Sergio Leone's classic westerns, *The Good The Bad And The Ugly*, *For A Few Dollars More* and *How The West Was Won*. Alex Cox first visited the site as a 17-year-old schoolboy and ardent fan of Leone. He had returned every year since, most impressed not by the celebrated Hollywood towns but by a little used set called Blanco Town, originally built for a Charles Bronson movie in 1972. "I always wanted to make a movie, in that place," he says.

Having written *The Legend Of Paddy Garcia* for The Pogues, Joe Strummer and a select clique of actors, Cox and Rude took the script to an agent called Jesse Beaton, who persuaded Island Pictures to cough up the one million dollar budget. After renaming the film *Straight To Hell* (a more 'full-on' title) cast and crew went into a low-pay partnership, and although Island own the

movie in the United States, it is Cox and Co who have the rights for the rest of the world.

Straight To Hell was unquestionably influenced by Sergio Leone but owed an even greater debt to Giulio Questi's *Django*. "Django was this spaghetti-western hero," explains Cox, "who'd get his hands cut off, have his neck broken or his tongue cut out; really terrible sadistic things would happen to him and yet he'd always triumph in the end. And *Straight To Hell* is actually ripped off *Django Kill*, which is the story of this horrible town where the townspeople are worse than the outlaws. It's full of lynchings, gratuitous sadism, cannibalism, homosexuality, and all kinds of good stuff."

It was The Pogues who were cast in *Hell* a Django-style townsfolk. They played the McMahons: a large clan who neither drink, smoke nor swear but suffer from terminal addiction to caffeine and killing. Under a formidable family motto of 'La Vida No Vale Nada' (Life Is Worth Nothing), they wreak trigger-happy havoc in Blanco Town: plundering Kaw-fee and annihilating strangers. Besides The Pogues and *Straight To Hell's* four stars – Joe Strummer, Courtney Love, Sy Richardson and Dick Rude – the cast was sprinkled with Grace Jones, Dennis Hopper and Amazulu.

Offset, Shane was becoming increasingly fascinated by the people and the place. He never tired of the Almerian mayhem, and was even prepared to swallow his vegetarian sensibilities and watch a bullfight. He also picked up on the Andalucian poet Federico Garcia De Lorca. "His poetry reads beautifully, and it was his area we were in. He was a popular poet in the same way that a lot of Irish poets were, in that he wrote in ballad form and wrote about what was going on among the people. His poetry doesn't come from intellectual thought, it comes from the connection between emotion and seeing and feeling. The other thing about him is that he was a faggot, and during the Civil War the fascists went round pulling out all the Republican sympathisers they could find, and

they got Lorca and shot him along with a lot of others, but because he was a faggot they rammed the gun up his arse and walked away laughing. But Lorca predicted his own death: he said that his body would disappear and that's exactly what happened and they never found it. He's a big folk hero in Spain and a brilliant poet."

The whole area seemed to emit a very strong sense of the dead. "You can feel it the same way as you can feel it in Ireland," says Shane. "All the hatred, all the suffering, all the blood, all the crazy dancing and singing – the soul of the country is still there." It was in Andalucia, using a Spanish guitar, that MacGowan wrote the beautiful ballad 'Lullaby Of London': 'May the winds that blow from

'Rake At The Gates Of Hell'. "They're both cowboy death songs which I wrote for the film. The whole idea of 'Rake At The Gates Of Hell' is very violent and romantic. It's the sort of thing that your classic maniac gunslinger would be thinking, about anybody who'd ever done anything to them, as they were waiting to go. It's inspired by Marty Robbins, you know, doom and death in the hot sun. And 'If I Should Fall From Grace With God' is inspired, I suppose, by gospel/country songs where they have one verse about God and the rest of it is about killing all the others."

Shot at buck-making pace, *Straight To Hell* was wrapped up in three and a half weeks. The sun scarred crew were exhausted, but the irrepressible director was already planning a *Back To Hell* follow-up.

On their return to Hitsville UK, The Pogues found themselves in the Top 40. MCA had lifted 'Haunted' from the *Sid 'n' Nancy: Love Kills* soundtrack and released it in single form on August 19. Whiffing the heavy scent of publicity, the banned 'Hot Dogs With Everything' was slapped on the B-side of the 12-inch. But lyrical obscenities failed to compensate for tame Pogues and 'Haunted' was slated by many of their fans. Packaged in the famous garbage scene still from *Sid 'n' Nancy* (and a back cover portrait of Cait), the band insisted that this wasn't The Pogues proper. "It was something that we did for the film and they decided to release it as a single. It wasn't really us," shrugs Spider.

'Haunted' failed to climb the charts and the band took a two-week break before going into rehearsal. Terry, Shane, Philip, James, Spider and Cait spent some of this time recording a charity LP with the London Irish Live Trust (LILT). Formed by Ron Kavana, LILT's main aim was to do a series of gigs under the general theme of a peaceful solution to Ireland's troubles through integration. Initially, LILT toyed with the possibility of setting up a trust for children orphaned as a direct result of the troubles but then they heard about the Belfast

haunted graves never bring you misery/May the angels bright watch you tonight and keep you while you sleep.'

"It's basically about a bloke being pissed, coming home and stumbling into his kid's bedroom," he explains. "The kid is freaking out, he's afraid of corncrakes and stuff like that, so the dad is just saying, 'Don't get fucked up; that hell and those demons have gone.' Obviously they haven't but you've got to say that to the kid or he'll be even more screwed up later on."

Although The Pogues had started the *Straight To Hell* filmscore back home, it was in Almeria that Shane composed 'If I Should Fall From Grace With God' and finished his delirious rhapsody

Charitable Trust For Integrated Education and saw it as the obvious channel.

After a successful benefit concert, LILT recorded seven of Kavana's songs under a collective title of 'Irish Ways – For The Children', and aimed to involve as many Irish artists in the project as possible. Consequently, the five Pogues played and sang on all the tracks, with Terry featuring on four and Shane singing the stand-out song 'Irish Ways (Callin' Me Home Again)'.

In the meantime, a European tour was lined up for November, but Darryl decided that although he might work with The Pogues in the future, he wanted to revert to playing himself. "In the early days of The Pogues," he says, "there was more of a camaraderie about everything. The six of them, with me driving and everyone mucking in together. But as the organization got bigger, I just ended up humping amplifiers around. Somebody has to do it, sure, but there seemed to be an ever decreasing circle of opportunities. And whereas everybody else, like Scully, had a job where they could express themselves, I had nothing apart from the odd chance to play bass."

It was 14 months since he had formed The Troubleshooters with Dave Scott and James' close friend and former Dolly Mixture, Debsey, and they were all keen to record a single and do regular gigs. After telling Frank that he had decided to leave, Darryl telephoned Joey Cashman and offered him his place. Joey took it.

Joe Cashman had first picked up a saxophone in 1978 and started playing in a series of bands in his native Dublin: The Fast Skirts, The Mod-1's and DC9 who achieved relative fame as Tokyo Olympics. Joey later got involved in film, working on a series of videos and building up his own portfolio.

On arriving back from The Pogues US tour Joey found work as a sound assistant on Alex Cox's *Straight To Hell*, and was biding his time for future film work when he was offered Darryl's position with The Pogues.

When the band returned to their Eezihire rehearsal space at the beginning of October, Cait failed to appear. So Jem asked Darryl, who was showing Joey the ropes, if he would fill in on bass. By the end of the first week, Frank had managed to contact Cait in Los Angeles where she was accompanying Elvis on tour. When Murray told her that she was required in London she coolly responded, "Send me a tape," but said she was on her way.

On October 9, Spider got married. His bride was Terri Lynn Moore, better known as Cheyne: the New Yorker who first captivated him some seven months before. Following the July tour of the States, Cheyne flew to Spain, and Spider proposed an immediate wedding. Anxious to avoid a Madonna/Penn spectacle, the couple opted for a private ceremony at Burnt Oak Registry Office which – since the other Pogues were in rehearsal – was attended by just Terry, Frank and Ferga. One minor detail was overlooked and the confetti had to be delayed while Murray dashed home for a cheque book. Their wedding afternoon was spent back at Eezihire (where James was celebrating his 32nd birthday) and their honeymoon in Camden Town.

Cait showed up the following week, but at the end of her second day she caused speculation by announcing that she was taking her bass home to practise. Two days later she called Murray from Los Angeles, and told him she would not be rejoining the band. Since Costello And The Attractions were to be on tour for several months, the news was hardly a surprise.

"I think the decision that she made is a normal decision for any man or woman to make," reasons Terry. "She actually faced up to the choice of being with the man she wanted to be with or being with the band, and when decisions get down to personal levels like that then I think personal life takes precedent."

And – with the exception of Shane – The Pogues accepted that Cait had made her final stand. "It was good that it happened when it did," says Jem, "'cos we'd only just started rehearsing. But I think it's better that someone leaves than hangs around without their heart in it. For a while you sometimes got the feeling that the heart wasn't there, and it would probably have become intolerable. Although it's still sad when someone that's been there from the start goes, especially in a band like this which was based on a group of friends."

Fortunately, there was Darryl, who was invited to return to the fold and command bass, at least until Christmas. Their European tour was to feature a completely revamped set and – with it now just three weeks away – they had a hurried go at the new material. This included 'Rake At The Gates Of Hell', 'If I Should Fall From Grace With God', 'Turkish Song Of The Damned', 'Lullaby Of London' (which they then recorded for a Janice Long session), a couple of Finer instrumentals and Terry singing the traditional 'South Australia' and a medley. An altogether more raucous and characteristically Pogues mix than the year's record would have indicated.

"We'd been playing the old set for ages, so it was really jaded," admits Shane. "There was a lot of quite complicated numbers in it from 'Rum, Sodomy And The Lash' so we just decided – well,

we didn't decide anything – but that's the way it came out 'cos we were all really pissed off with the old one."

At the same time, MacGowan bought a bouzouki (which cost £100 and took one minute to tune) and set to work on a series of new numbers. "The bouzouki is a very easy instrument to play," he says. "You can play three times as fast as a guitar player, so it takes all the bullshit out of being a guitarist and I found that I could play practically anything on it."

Their new set was to include 'The Broad Majestic Shannon', the ballad written for Tommy Makem and Liam Clancy; and they simultaneously worked out a jazz funk song, 'Driving Through The City', which Shane wrote for Grace Jones while they were filming *Straight To Hell*.

Meanwhile, Christy Moore – who had always been acknowledged, alongside The Dubliners and Clancy Brothers, as The Pogues' greatest influence – began a major tour of England. Among his own gems was an interpretation of 'A Pair Of Brown Eyes'. "This," he told his audience, "is a song written by my new hero: young MacGowan out of The Pogues."

Joey Cashman with James Fearnley

The end of the month also provided a rare privilege. The Dubliners, recording a double LP to commemorate their 25th anniversary, asked The Pogues to guest on a couple of tracks. Their kindred soul was consequently united in Elephant Studios on October 29 and 30. The chosen songs were 'The Irish Rover' and 'The Rare Auld Mountain Dew', with MacGowan and Ronnie Drew splitting the vocals. "I never had to sing as fast in my life!" says Ronnie.

Both tracks were produced by Eamonn Campbell who had been involved with The Dubliners since the late sixties, and had been particularly close to the late Luke Kelly. Flayed by the strains of 'Rum, Sodomy And The Lash', Eamonn told his son Paddy, "I'd love to produce for that band" – a year later The Dubliners were giving him the opportunity.

"I must admit that I felt apprehensive," says Eamonn, "especially when I walked into Elephant Studios and there were 14 people there. But it turned out to be the best thing I've ever produced. They're a great bunch of lads; the finest you could meet."

The Pogues and Dubliners were equally elated by the finished tape, which more than matched the occasion. "Tex Mex," glowed Terry on hearing 'The Rare Auld Mountain Dew'. "No," quipped Shane, "Tick Micks." "I think The Dubliners understand us and we understand them," says MacGowan. "We both take the piss out of ourselves but we both take the music seriously in the end."

The following Tuesday, it was back to hell: this time for 23 dates in France, Germany, Switzerland, Belgium and Holland. The tour began as it was to continue, when – with lost echoes of the Finnjet Ferry – Spider and DJ collapsed from the bar into their cabin berths. On reaching French soil, no amount of knocking could waken them and The Pogues had no choice but to face their Brest audience without a whistle-player and with the monitors left to chance.

The errant pair managed to make it to the second night in Saint-Malo, but two days later the whole party failed to arrive in Berlin. As the hours ticked by the German tour manager (whose last encounter with The Pogues led to a nervous breakdown) steeled himself to the fact that the band were going to miss their first and most important date.

Shane and The Dubliners, October 1986

It turned out that there had been a serious error in the tour itinerary and consequently – through no fault of their own – The Pogues had missed the flight to Berlin. There was no alternative but to take another two days off, and fly directly to the next gig in Hamburg instead.

The tour hit a highspot, on November 14 in Munich, when The Dubliners joined The Pogues for an encore of 'The Irish Rover', 'The Rare Auld Mountain Dew' and 'The Wild Rover'. The audience responded with a shower of well-intentioned missiles. These included several shoes, one of which scored a direct – and very painful – hit in Andrew's crotch. "The whole thing was just mad," remembers Spider.

"The Dubliners, in lots of ways, were Pogues

111

before The Pogues," says Terry. "The only thing that I sadly miss about working with them is that Luke Kelly isn't around. Luke was a particular friend. Every Saturday we'd play football together in Dartmouth Square. We'd play amongst ourselves, but there was always a match."

Early the next morning, The Pogues dragged themselves back to their coach and made for Zurich. After a bleary-brained pitstop at a service station, they continued the journey southward. But, on reaching the Austrian border, it was discovered that although Joey's ubiquitous leather jacket was present, Cashman himself was not to be found. Joey – increasingly useful since he could

already distinguish between a mandola and a mandolin – had been left in the service station with only a pair of jeans and a Sandinista sweatshirt to his name.

There was nothing for it but to retrieve the wanderer. So, while The Pogues piled into a nearby restaurant, the coach backtracked to Munich. Three hours later, the driver returned without Joey, and another six hours passed before Cashman eventually turned up in a state-sponsored taxi; having spent the best part of the day in a Bavarian police station.

A mad dash through Switzerland followed, with The Pogues finally reaching Zurich some two hours after their scheduled show, but still managing to satisfy the disgruntled crowd with a belated burst of 'The Irish Rover' and a very dicey set.

In the third week, it was back to France for another nine dates, including a Southern stint in Nice, Montpellier and Toulouse. By this time, most of the problems with their new set had been overcome, and Toulouse saw one of their best performances of the tour. But it also came dangerously close to being their last.

Heading towards their hotel in the post-midnight hours of that rainy, windswept night, the coach got stuck on a narrow country lane. The driver attempted to forge their way through but, seconds later, everyone clutched in mild horror as they felt themselves slowly begin to topple. Miraculously the fall stopped at a precarious 45 degrees, where they remained until a repair service towed the coach upright.

The trek reached its summit in Paris, on November 24, when they played to 4,000 people at Le Zenith. In just 12 months, their Parisian audience had increased more than tenfold, and The Pogues were surrounded by press and fans alike. "That tour turned out to be an even bigger sell-out than ever," says Terry. "Which is surprising when you consider that we should have had an album out but didn't."

After Paris, they descended into the pits of Rennes, Rouen and Le Mans. The latter show was marred by a bunch of sieg-heiling fascists who, in a scene reminiscent of Hitler's 1985 birthday celebrations in Berlin, insisted on making their presence felt. The Pogues met them with verbal challenge and, when the rest of the crowd backed the band, the minority bleated out.

The remainder of the tour brought four nights in Belgium and Holland. Their penultimate date in Deinze, just south of Ghent, was to have been attended by two coachloads from London. The trip was organized by the Brighton-based Mead Gould Promotions, with concert ticket and return

journey at an all-inclusive price of £45. But one of the coaches never made it to Belgium. It was turned back en route when the promoter decided the entourage were too drunk to continue. This was denied by angry fans who were not given a refund; but the press were quick to reflect the incident on "Ireland's booze/rock" Pogues.

By the last night in Utrecht, a month on the road had taken its toll, and everyone was desperate for home. "Sometimes it's just complete hell," says Andrew. "It's always really exhausting, so you have to cope with that to begin with. But it's not just the physical demands, a lot of the time you're really fucked up in your head too: you don't know where you are, you don't know why you're there, you're fed up with all these complete arseholes that you have to deal with, you're lonely and you're bored. I mean, the bad side of it is really bad – it's worse than anything I've ever done and I've done some pretty vile jobs in the past. But the good side of it is much better, and also you know that you just have to do it, and somehow or other you get through. You may play like a pile of shit, but you still do the gigs, and the more you do the better you get at doing it."

Back from hell, but not for long. The Pogues were given 36 hours before starting another round of England, Scotland and Ireland. Terry escaped to Cavan to celebrate his birthday with his family but, whatever happened next, the band decided that this tour would be followed by a three-week break.

cular. But while Frank Murray seethed backstage, neither audience nor press appeared to notice: downstairs was a delirious jungle of heads, arms, shoulders, scarves and Tricolours; and the papers followed with rave reviews.

"It's great, actually, the support we've got for someone who hasn't really put a record out all year," says Jem. "But I don't know how we got away with that one. If I'd been reviewing it, then I'd really have laid into us."

Following two sold-out shows at the Hammersmith Palais, Shane paid a flying visit to Dublin to be photographed with Ronnie Drew for the Christmas cover of *Hot Press*. He was driven from the airport to the photo-session and quickly back to the airport by The Pogues' Irish publicist Terry O'Neill. After dropping MacGowan off the car was involved in a serious collision and, although O'Neill escaped with reparable damage, the passenger side was a total write-off. Shane returned to London, mercifully unaware.

In Glasgow, The Pogues popularity had never been in doubt and their return to Barrowlands on December 12-13 gave the Ballroom a new attendance record. By 7.00 pm, Gallowgate was alive with music. Tonight it wasn't the usual Saturday sing-a-longs, but the songs of MacGowan arranged by all and sundry. Amid the unwearying strains of 'Sick Bed', 'Brown Eyes' and 'Sally MacLennane' in the Barrowlands Bar, was Sean Conboy who had travelled from Birmingham for his 74th Pogues gig.

When The Pogues hit the boards, Barrowlands was more impressive than ever: a fanatical forest of green and white, stretching and spreading and finally engulfing the entire ballroom, and reverberating every chorus from 'The Irish Rover' to the wild one. The crowd's fervour was not without its drawbacks. The scene was interpreted by some as an open celebration of sectarianism, a view further emphasised by the sight of a bloodied Rangers fan.

This put The Pogues in a precarious position

"I've got to spend some time at home," said Terry. "I haven't been home since October, which isn't the easiest way to have a family. So I personally need a few weeks just to sort out my home life and reasssure the children. That's the nice thing about this band: with all its abnormalities, it has a sense of normality that is very prevalent."

The Back From Hell Tour got underway, on December 4, in the stately surrounds of Kilburn's National Ballroom. It was The Pogues first London appearance in nine months and, not surprisingly, saw a haze of publicity, a guest list of 500 (Cait and Elvis among them) and a sea of green flooding to its tinselled rafters.

First night nerves were increased by sound problems and the show itself was far from specta-

even though they collectively spanned a broad religious spectrum (from pagan to agnostic to lapsed Catholic) and had done little to incite such passion other than play what was essentially Irish-based music and simply be The Pogues. Ironically enough, the band returned to their hotel to find that Rangers Football Club had chosen the same venue for their Christmas party.

Five days later they were bound for Holyhead, and the final leg of Back From Hell. It was to be The Pogues first Irish date since Self-Aid and a visit to which everybody had been looking forward.

Their first date was a sold-out show at Dublin's Olympic. The majority of the crowd were as pant mayhem. The majority of the crowd were as drunk as they were young, and it took complete darkness and an intro-loop of 'Year Of The French' to hush them into any kind of order.

With just a minute to go, Paul Scully shrieked in disbelief from the sound desk. Somebody had run a dastardly hand across the controls and, in one second, had laid waste a two-hour sound check. That was only the beginning: he spent the next 70 minutes mopping a continual spray of beer from his precious equipment.

But if the Olympic proved a nightmare for Scully and the Pogue sound, the audience were unperturbed. They sang along with inspired ardour and, during 'Dirty Old Town' and 'The Auld Triangle', the band was barely audible at all.

The following night saw another sell-out and further madness at the SFX, though a late-night session at the Pogues' spiritual home, Blooms Hotel, proved more entertaining than the actual gig.

Dublin was the best place in the world for The Finnish Rover (a Guinness and vodka cocktail invented by MacGowan) and there was no bar where it tasted like this. After several Rovers, Eamonn Campbell produced his guitar and led James, Jem and an increasing circle of Irish musicians through 'That's Alright Mama', 'His Latest Flame' and 'Peggy Gordon', while Shane poured the essence of Luke Kelly into 'Dirty Old Town'.

"Shane sang that for me," smiles Eamonn, "Luke was my best friend. I was with him when he died, and carried his coffin. And it meant the world to me just to hear Shane singing his song."

The songs went on for several rounds, and Blooms was packed until dawn. This was to be the last day of the tour, and The Dubliners were scheduled for a guest appearance at The Pogues' final show in Dun Laoghaire.

In the afternoon, however, Shane – who never seemed to sleep before noon – emerged with a severely gashed nose, the result of an early morning fracas involving a basketball player, a Blooms' dustbin and the MacGowan charisma. In the absence of a make-up artist, PV promised to go easy on the stage lights.

The venue was an old dancehall, The Top Hat, and Back From Hell hit the ultimate end when The Dubliners appeared for a second encore of 'The Rare Old Mountain Dew' and 'The Irish Rover'. By the time they entered the third round with 'The Wild Rover', there were 19 Pogues on stage: Frank, Cheyne and Paul Scully's son Robin dived for drums, lensman Tom Collins grabbed a mike and even PV abandoned his lightshow.

"I enjoyed it tremendously," says Ronnie Drew. "I thought all the young kids would be wondering what the auld fellows were doing up there, but they didn't. It was marvellous."

The band took a three-week Christmas break but were back in Dublin on January 13 for a TV appearance on *Mega Mix*. Then it was back to rehearsal until February 3 when they started recording the soundtrack for *Straight To Hell*.

With Paul Scully and Dave Jordan producing, they slapped down 'Rake At The Gates Of Hell', 'If I Should Fall From Grace With God', an instrumental titled 'Rabinga' and a cover of 'The Good The Bad And The Ugly'. The latter was to be the title track but it turned out to be so faithful to the original that it was pointless. After a couple of

115

wrought suggestions, Jem said that they should record a hip hop version instead. With the notable exception of DJ and James, there was little enthusiasm for Finer's notion until Andrew telephoned to say that he couldn't make it to the studio and they had no choice but to use a drum machine. The resulting track was topped up with cider-fuelled shrieks, slabs of heavy metal guitar and wholesale pickings from the Morricone original, and later mixed with bits from the previous day's recording.

In the meantime, The Pogues had been given another screen role in the Comic Strip's *Eat The Rich*: a black comedy featuring middle-aged anarchists and minced-up yuppies. The star-strewn cast included the Comic Strip regulars plus Fiona Richmond, Motorhead, Paul McCartney, Sandie Shaw, Bill Wyman, Koo Stark, Jools Holland and Hugh Cornwell. Shane, Terry, Frank and Spider grabbed cameo roles as a bunch of terrorists (and a Celtic scarved journalist), while Joey worked on the sound team.

Although The Pogues were ready to start recording their third LP, Frank Murray was no longer prepared for it to be released on Stiff. He believed that – despite Dave Robinson's claims to the contrary – their floundering label did not have the finances to back such an important record.

Consequently February was 28 days of hanging around. "It was a real drag," says James. "I'd thought, 'This is the year when everything is going to happen' and suddenly there was bugger all going on. It was like waiting for a bus – you know it's going to come but you don't know when."

March 6 brought the first rumble when The Pogues flew to Dublin for a special edition of *The Late Late Show*. It was a night for tall tales and great voices as The Pogues, U2, Christy Moore, The Fureys, Stockton's Wing, Jim McCann and even Taoiseach Charlie Haughey helped Ronnie Drew, Barney MacKenna, John Sheahan, Sean Cannon and Eamonn Campbell to celebrate 25 years of The Dubliners.

There was rare footage of the late Luke Kelly singing 'Scorn Not His Simplicity', an emotive rendition of 'Springhill Mining Disaster' from U2, Christy Moore belting out 'The Black Velvet Band' and The Pogues teaming with The Dubliners and Christy for 'The Irish Rover'. But the highlight came when Ciaran Bourke (now semi-paralysed through illness) recited a tribute to Brendan Behan and the entire cast echoed 'The Auld Triangle'. "The whole thing was really moving – it just sent shivers down your spine," says Jem, "and I think we all felt really proud to be there."

After a night of the usual in Blooms, The Pogues returned to London and started preparing for Saint Patrick's Day: when they were to play in front of a crowd of 5,000 at Brixton Academy.

Keen for a novelty factor, on this their fourth annual show, someone suggested that they should hire the appropriate gear and pose as New York police vets. The idea was quickly agreed and Andrew and PV set to work on a huge backdrop of the Manhattan City skyline.

"I didn't like the idea when it first came up," says James. "I thought the idea of dressing up as police was too macho, and I do worry about what else something means apart from looking good. Ever since Cait left I've been really aware of The Pogues being all blokes, although I'm not too worried so long as, as a group, we don't start pushing forward male attitudes."

The band built up to the 17th with a hat-trick of Round Saint Patrick's dates and it was during this period that Murray recruited a new backliner and Pogue called Charlie MacLennon. Better known as Big Charlie, he started working with Alex Harvey in 1968, toured with Thin Lizzy – as personal manager to Phil Lynott – throughout the seventies, and had spent the last five years working for Joan Armatrading.

The Pogues opened and closed their Saint Patrick's Day sets with 'The Irish Rover' and chose the big day itself to release the version which they

St. Patrick's gig – 1987

had recorded with The Dubliners, and which had been remixed by Dave Jordan.

By the following week, 'The Irish Rover' had shot straight into the Top 40. But before the charts were announced, Spider was making his way to Nicaragua. He was to appear alongside Joe Strummer, Dick Rude and a host of other *Straight To Hell* stars in Alex Cox's *Walker* – a film documenting the life and times of William Walker, the American soldier who declared himself President of Nicaragua in 1855.

While Stacy flew to South America, his colleagues headed back to Ireland to co-star with The Dubliners on the *Tom O'Connor Roadshow*. They arrived in Derry on the eve of the show, drank their way through to the morning and made a bleary-eyed lunchtime appearance in the Town Hall.

Afterwards the Lord Mayor invited the bands to have a drink in his plush chamber. What he failed to account for was both the size of their ever-increasing entourage and their limitless capacity for alcohol. "I suppose he meant a civilized drink," smiles Jem, "but he had loads of bottles of spirits and there was all of us, The Dubliners, and people like the writer Eamonn McCann, and I think he bit off more than he could chew."

The afternoon tipple rapidly evolved into a fully fledged session with drink, music and more drink. But it was a Brendan Behan song which finally proved too much for the Mayor. As 'the auld triangle went jingle jangle' he threw off his civic chain and fled the building.

Several hours later, Terry Woods, Ronnie Drew and Barney MacKenna decided to make their way to Dublin and Barney – who was the most sober of the three – was nominated to take the wheel. MacKenna failed to realize that the car was an automatic and mistook the brake for the clutch several times.

Not surprisingly, they were barely 200 yards down the road when the RUC pulled them over and, without bothering with the breathalizer, carted them off for a night in the cells. Waking in the early hours of the next morning, Ronnie turned to Barney and in all seriousness enquired, "What sort of fucken' hotel is this?"

"You're not in a hotel, you're in the cells," returned Barney, before sniping. "Sing 'The Auld Triangle' now, you little bollocks."

The trio managed to find alternative accommodation for the following weekend, when the two bands blasted *Saturday Live* with 'The Irish Rover'. By a neat quirk of coincidence, the show was hosted by Ben Elton – the same presenter who, three years before, had suggested to *South Of Watford* viewers that The Pogues were destined to play The Hope And Anchor *ad infinitum*. But, this time round, Elton gave the band an unashamed and long overdue plug.

Three days later, 'The Irish Rover' was touching on the Top 20 and they were invited to appear on *Top Of The Pops*.

Lining up alongside Curiosity Killed The Cat, The Pogues and their bearded mentors were as

novel a bunch of pop toppers as the BBC was likely to get and – when they took the stage for rehearsal – the entire floor crew burst into applause. "This place has changed a fair bit since I was last here," remarked Ronnie Drew, as he cast an eye around Studio Six. "When was that?" asked the floor manager. "1967," replied Ronnie, to general laughter.

The Dubliners bridged the wait in their 20-year gap in the BBC Club (where they were admirably entertained by the barman and his vast repertoire of John McCormack songs) before being herded back to Studio Six where a BBC executive was urging the 'live' audience to enjoy themselves and shooing the best dressed ones in front of the cameras and, at 7.00 pm, it was time for Janice Long to beam in the 'big surprise'.

After the show, the champagne flowed freer than ever and, by the following week, 'The Irish Rover' had risen to number eight. "*Top Of The Pops* was a laugh," says Jem, "but personally I found the show and the whole thing of being in the Top 10 quite meaningless."

Something that meant more, to Shane at least, was the single simultaneously reaching number one in Ireland. The band marked their achievement with an Easter appearance at Dublin's Gaiety Theatre.

They flew across on Saturday, had a quick rehearsal on Sunday afternoon and were to be televised live on RTE at 10.00pm. But five minutes before they were due on stage, it suddenly occurred to Frank that not only was Jem missing but he wasn't going to turn up. A last second reshuffle ensued with Terry grabbing Jem's banjo and passing his own cittern to the attendant Philip Donnelly.

Afterwards, they returned to Blooms Bar – where they found Finer. Apparently, he had gone for a post-rehearsal drink with Shane, decided on a quick kip in his room and eventually awoke at 11.58pm. "It was all dark and I couldn't work out where I was," says Jem. "Then it dawned on me

Charlie MacLennon with Shane

that I'd gone to sleep at six o'clock and the television show had been at 10. At first I thought, 'Oh no!' Then I just burst into hysterical laughter because it was all so completely absurd. I'd gone all the way to Dublin, done the rehearsal but missed the whole caboodle. So I just went downstairs to the bar and everyone came back and laughed at me."

The band spent the following weekend in France. They were billed to support James Brown at a festival in Bourges, but the Godfather pulled out at the last moment and The Pogues ended up headlining over Trouble Funk and Johnny Clegg.

Spider was to have joined them in Paris, but was delayed in Nicaragua and flown back to London a week later instead. He had spent the past six weeks in Managua and Granada, in the screen role of a mercenary. "I was just sort of being there," he shrugs. "I got punched in the face, clubbed over the head with a pistol; pulled a sword on some Nicaraguans and marched the President to his execution – and eventually got to die of cholera."

While he was there, though, Spider was inspired to write a song, full of pride and passion, which

Steve Lillywhite, Kirsty and Strummer

he tentatively titled 'Walk Tall Nicaragua' and which he sang to the tune (or thereabouts) of 'James Connelly'. "One of the things that I sensed really strongly was that the Nicaraguan people have suffered for a long time under a repressive government, and also endured all sorts of other problems, like earthquakes. And now that they've got rid of their dictator and are trying to do something for themselves, they're being bullied by the Americans. But, even if the Americans invade and take all the major cities, those people will never surrender: they'll just shoot the stars and stripes to shreds."

Straight To Hell was scheduled for June release and, by way of a byline, Frank asked Def Jam supremo Rick Rubin to remix their hip hop version of 'The Good The Bad And The Ugly'. Rubin, however, failed to share their enthusiasm for the track: he said that the tempo was more disco than hip hop and suggested that they slow it down by using a heavy metal drummer.

Brian Downey, of Thin Lizzy renown, subsequently laid down a drum solo, and the track was mixed at Elephant Studios by Dave Jordan. "Brian did an excellent job," says DJ, "but when Jem said, 'Let's do a hip hop version' he had as much idea about hip hop as anybody else. And, by doing exactly what Rick Rubin told us to do, I think we completely missed the point. What we had in the first place was a great track – it was completely mental but it was definitely The Pogues."

By this time the ongoing discussions between The Pogues and their record company had broken down completely and, in order to keep Stiff's hands off the record, they decided to pay for the recording themselves.

Consequently, on May 9, they started recording their new LP at last. The venue was RAK Studio in London's Saint John's Wood and the producer was Steve Lillywhite. Lillywhite, who had climbed his way up through the studio ranks (from teaboy to engineer to producer) had worked with a whole series of Celtic bands including U2, Simple Minds, Big Country and, of course, his wife Kirsty MacColl.

It was while he was in Dublin, doing some remixes on U2's 'The Joshua Tree', that he met up with Murray and casually asked who was producing the next Pogues LP. Murray had replied, "We don't know. Do you want to do it?"

Recording went like a dream: in the first week they laid seven backing tracks and after just 11 days the first half of the record was almost completed. "Waiting around for four months was really frustrating and, in a way, quite demoralizing," says Jem, "but as soon as we got into the studio everyone really leapt at it. And – without slagging off our previous producers – having an actual producer rather than a musician producing has made an incredible difference. Steve doesn't mess around with the arrangements he just gets them to sound the best they possibly can."

The band's enthusiasm and respect for Lillywhite was more than reciprocated. "The thing about The Pogues is that you can't really compare them with any other groups," says Steve. "There's so many people and so many different influences; James' influences, for example, don't come anywhere near where Shane's influences come from and Jem gets it all completely different again. But, at the same time, they're very much a band and I always tend to do my best work when I'm working within a family type configuration. They've also got a very definite idea about how the songs should sound, and I'm just here putting it all to bed."

Although there were a number of differences between these Pogues and those who had recorded 'Rum, Sodomy And The Lash' – Darryl, Philip (and Andrew on a full rather than a two-piece kit) – the most significant addition was Terry Woods. He gave the band an extra dimension both in terms of the arrangements and the songs themselves.

Himself and Shane had worked out a startling number, tracing several centuries of Irish oppression and injustice. It begins with the lament like strains of Woods' 'Streets Of Sorrow', which refers in particular to the Irish revolutionary Michael Collins, and builds into the murderous incomprehension of MacGowan's 'Birmingham Six': 'There were six men in Birmingham and in Guildford there's four/that were picked up and tortured and framed by the law/ and the filth got promotion but they're still doing time/ for being Irish in the wrong place and at the wrong time . . ./ You'll be counting years, first five, then 10/ growing old in a lonely hell/ round the yard and the stinking cell/ from wall to wall, and back again.'

"It's about people getting framed up by the British system of justice, or whatever you want to call it," says Shane. "It specifically mentions the Birmingham Six and the Guildford Four but there's also a verse about the eight guys who were recently done by the SAS. Basically, it's about anybody who's been locked up without any real evidence against them."

Among the other new songs was the tacky summer sound of 'Fiesta', jazzed up with a brass section of Joey Cashman, After Tonite's Eli Thompson and Brian Clarke, and former Pride Of The Cross man Paul Taylor. Jem had based the tune on Almeria's infamous Chochona song, while some of MacGowan's lyrics were a paraphrase of Lorcas's 'Ballad Of The Accursed': 'El veinticino de agosto, abrio sus ojos Jaime Fearnley . . ./Y Costello el rey del America y suntuosa Cait O'Riordan.' "It's just about a bunch of wankers going to Spain during the summer," shrugs Shane.

At the end of May, Steve Lillywhite had to forsake The Pogues to produce Talking Heads in Paris, but Murray had already lined up a busy 10 days in Ireland. Their first destination was Cork, where they were to be filmed by a French TV crew for the prestigious *Johnny Hallyday Show*. But the weekend turned into a complete farce when they were driven all the way to Killarney, merely to sit in a pub and mime to 'Sally MacLennane'.

From Killarney it was up the country to Dublin to host an RTE TV special. The Pogues' invited guests were naturally enough The Dubliners and, as a special aside, Joe Strummer was there to perform a couple of songs with Terry. But when it was time for Strummer's spot, the rest of the band persuaded him to let them play too and a raucous mix of 'I Fought The Law' and 'London Calling' ensued. The Pogues own performance was, however, wrecked by an uncharacteristic spasm of nerves and the recording needed serious surgery before it hit the air.

After consecutive weekends in Kenmare and Bremen, The Pogues returned to London to attend the première of *Straight To Hell*. The movie had already been slated by most of the critics: *Filmnight*'s Barry Norman had commented, "It took Alex Cox and Dick Rude three and a half days to write this script. Frankly, I'm amazed it took them so long."

But *Straight To Hell*'s star and self-proclaimed publicist Courtney Love deflected the flak with, "If you don't like obnoxious children and you don't like dogs that piss on your carpet and you haven't got a sense of humour then you're not going to like *Straight To Hell*."

Two days later, The Pogues faced a crowd of 70,000 when they were lined up with Lone Justice and Lou Reed, as support to U2 at Wembley Stadium. The next six weeks continued in similar style with further U2 dates in Dublin's Croke Park and Paris' L'Hippodrome, followed by a week of festivals in Italy and Finland.

On July 18, the band staged a Picnic In The Park, in London's Finsbury Park, but it rained throughout the afternoon and the event proved more of a Glastonbury mudbath than a picnic. Nevertheless The Pogues attracted a crowd of 8,000 and the melée of stumbling bodies, flying shoes and ripped clothing was more exuberant than ever.

The following Monday, The Pogues were back

in RAK Studio and managed to lay eight backing tracks in a matter of days. Among the new material was 'Thousands Are Sailing', a Philip Chevron number, linking the current exodus of young Irish men and women to America with the mass flights of the past. Written in the same vein as his Radiators' classic 'Faithful Departed', Chevron managed to capture all the dreams, fears and tears of the reluctant exile. 'In Manhattan's desert twilight in the death of afternoon/ we stood hand in hand on Broadway like the first men on the moon/ and 'The Blackbird' broke the silence as you whistled it so sweet/ and in Brendan Behan's footsteps I danced up and down the street . . ./ And we raised a glass to JFK and a dozen more besides/ when I got back to my empty room I suppose I must have cried.'

Meanwhile, MacGowan had come up with 'Sit Down By The Fire' and collaborated with Finer on 'Bottle Of Smoke'. The former is a late night tale that revs into a rampant jig and tempers the spooks and ghouls with the vintage refrain 'Good night and God bless, now fuck off to bed.' "It's the kind of story they tell you before you go to bed, just to freak you out completely," says Shane. "It's about all the things that can get you in the old, creaking house as you lay there in the dark. It's a typical Irish bedtime story."

'Bottle Of Smoke', on the other hand, is a glorious commentary on an unfancied racehorse. "It's basically about the Cheltenham Gold Cup," says MacGowan, "going to the races and betting a lot of money on an outsider. But it wins, of course, otherwise people would accuse us of being pessimists. With a name like 'Bottle Of Smoke' how could it lose?"

The Pogues had also come up with three new instrumentals: Woods' 'The Battle March', MacGowan's 'The Ballinalee' and a Carolan-type tune which was referred to simply as 'The Instrumental' but which Shane had privately christened 'Shanne Bradley'. "It's a tune which I made up on the bouzouki a few months ago," he says. "Carolan

used to write songs for men and songs for women, and sometimes he wrote them for himself, like 'The Ode To Whiskey'. But generally they were for a patron or someone that he was obsessed with or loved. And this is just a very graceful tune, which is named after the woman that I was thinking about at the time."

For the next six weeks, the band recorded from Monday to Thursday and gigged at the weekends. Their dates included a headline spot (over Chuck Berry) in Geneva and a place on U2's Edinburgh bill. "The Pogues write great songs and make brilliant music," said their bassist Adam Clayton, "and we're delighted to have them with us."

Although U2 wound up their three-month European tour at the Cork Festival, it was The Dubliners and not The Pogues who were chosen to support them. The Pogues played on the following day's bill – with Christy Moore, The Wolftones and Status Quo – but turned in a less than perfect performance, and Shane was particularly slated for forgetting the words to 'A Pair Of Brown Eyes'.

In the studio, however, MacGowan sang each song like it was his last. With Steve Lillywhite at the controls, he shot 'If I Should Fall From Grace With God' with a new vitality and transformed Chevron's 'Thousands Are Sailing' into his own.

"Certain people are special," says DJ, "and special people when they're on form are devastating. And that's the way Shane is. Most of the time I just think . . .'Wanker' but when he really goes for it, he's something else."

MacGowan's Cork blunders had already been forgotten by the time the band returned to Ireland, on August 23, to headline the Tralee Festival where they were billed under the ridiculous heading of 'The Unique Shane MacGowan And The Pogues'.

While most of them proved consistent losers at the races, the unique one got lucky with a visit from the reigning Rose – who was gracious enough to sign their postcard to Tom Waits. Waits

– a Rose Of Tralee advocate since 'Rain Dogs' and before – had just released the studio version of 'Franks Wild Years' and was plugging The Pogues as his favourite band. "I love The Pogues," he said. "Like out of a Hieronymous Bosch painting. Mythic. Mystical. In their very own drunken fashion."

Back at RAK, Shane shared vocals with Kirsty MacColl to capture 'Fairytale Of New York' on record at last. Set in a New York drunk tank on Christmas Eve, it's the story of an old couple, bound by indelible memories and living on un-utterable dreams. 'I could have been someone,' whines Shane. 'So could anyone,' retorts Kirsty, 'You took my dreams from me when I first found you.' 'I kept them with me babe,' he sighs, 'and put them with my own, can't make it all alone, I've built my dreams around you.'

With its bells, Broadway and thoughts as distant as Galway Bay, 'Fairytale Of New York' sounded like the Christmas record to end them all. The Pogues final recording was 'Worms': a 45-second fairy tale of an entirely different kind, rasped by Ranken and accompanied by Fearnley.

This time round, the band's problem was not what to put on the LP but what to leave off. "Steve seems to have brought out the best in all of us," enthuses Philip. "He realized at the very beginning that we are highly individualized, and I can't think of any other producer who'd have been able to get the same results."

On completing the LP, Steve Lillywhite flew to New York to resume production duties with Talking Heads. But within three weeks The Pogues had landed two support slots to U2, at Boston's Sullivan Stadium and New York's Madison Square Garden, and Lillywhite subse-quently asked James and Terry to guest on Talking Heads eclectic 'Naked'.

The Pogues themselves attracted the attention of everyone from Faye Dunaway to The Beastie Boys and Los Lobos. "You guys are like the Hell's Angels," declared MTV director Peter Dougherty. "Everyone wants to hang out with you but nobody wants to give you their home address."

During this period, The Pogues learned that Dave Robinson had served legal writs in order to gain possession of their LP tapes. To compli-cate the matter still further, Frank Murray received a call from Island Records' Chris Blackwell saying that he wanted to buy the band out of their Stiff contract. The terms of a deal were quickly agreed but, by the time they supported U2 at Madison Square Garden, the deal was off.

On October 16, the battle between The Pogues and Stiff Records reached the High Court. But half an hour before their case was due to be heard Stiff stopped the writ. Dave Robinson had resigned as MD and was replaced by Chris O'Donnell who, unlike his predecessor, was able to form a good working relationship with Frank Murray.

It was decided that The Pogues should have their own record label and 'Fairytale Of New York' subsequently appeared on Pogue Mahone, pressed and distributed by EMI, and the band later negotiated a US deal with Island.

While 'Fairytale Of New York' was coupled with 'The Battle March Medley'/'Shanne Bradley' and rush released for Christmas, the band toyed with the titles 'Fiesta' and 'Pogue Mahone' but finally christened the LP 'If I Should Fall From Grace With God'.

In the meantime they returned to the road with a seven-date jaunt around Ireland under the Na Gopaleen banner of The Brother Wouldn't Look At An Egg. The trek included two nights in Terry Woods' home town of Virginia, County Cavan, and the entire population turned up at The Lake Hotel to catch their resident Pogue in action.

Their Irish dates were followed by a one-off London date at Camden's Electric Ballroom, where a shambolic set was enlivened by a Joe Strummer encore of 'I Fought The Law' and 'London Calling'.

By this time, Philip Chevron was suffering from

severe ulcer trouble and, on doctor's orders, agreed to drop out of their American tour. Frank Murray called the first guitarist he could think of. "It was funny the way it happened," smiles Joe Strummer. "I'd met Jimmy The Red, a well known drinker around Notting Hill, and he was telling me that he'd been to Narcotics Anonymous, had given up everything and was feeling great. So I decided to knock drinking on the head for a month, went home and was sat there feeling all smug with my new decision when the phone rang and Frank Murray said, 'Joe, you're gonna come to New York with us in three days time'."

Strummer's resolution was short-lived indeed when, on arriving in New York, The Pogues were driven to a downtown drunk tank to record a 'Fairytale' video. The real action began when the boys of the NYPD decided that the entourage weren't as sober as a film crew should be. But director Peter Dougherty managed to save the band from a night in the tank by propping Charlie (who was acting as Santa Claus) against a sturdy counter and getting Matt Dillon to guide Shane up a potentially precarious staircase.

The three-week tour took in Canada and the States, and culminated in two West coast dates with Los Lobos. "There's something about thrashing an instrument to the limit," says Strummer, "and what really appeals to me about The Pogues is the sheer physicality of the music. I loved the way we could really rock the house with a tiny little thing like a mandolin, rather than bludgeoning the audience into submission with a huge wall of sound. On 'Medley' we'd all gather round Terry Woods and he'd raise one eyebrow which was the signal to go double time . . . it was scary enough just to learn all that stuff let alone try and play it at 900 miles per hour."

Despite MacGowan's Radio One anomalies of 'You scum bag, you maggott, you cheap lousy faggott/ Happy Christmas your arse, I pray God it's our last,' by the time The Pogues returned to London they were on course for a yuletide number one. They even changed the lyrics to 'Happy Christmas, you ass' in order to appear on *Top Of The Pops* but were beaten to the post by the Pet Shop Boys cover of 'Always On My Mind'.

In Ireland, though, 'Fairytale Of New York' was an easy winner with even JP Donleavy now keen to meet MacGowan. The single topped the charts throughout January and the LP followed suit.

Since 'Poguetry In Motion' almost two years before, The Pogues vinyl silence had been shattered only by 'The Irish Rover' and 'Fairytale', 'Haunted' didn't count, both of which owed much of their success to sheer novelty. But, released on January 18 1988, 'If I Should Fall From Grace With God' was ample evidence of The Pogues widening scope and musical capabilities.

The record was a thunderous concoction of just about every roots style from folk, country and western, jazz and rock to Irish, Latin and an eccentric taste of the East. The latter influences are best exemplified by the dual MacGowan/Finer compositions 'Fiesta' and 'Turkish Song Of The Damned', while Finer shot a traditional Irish melody with hellbent jazz to turn 'Metropolis' into a bizarre variation of the *Miami Vice* theme.

While the increasing instrumental capacity of James Fearnley shone through Steve Lillywhite's production, the calibre of other Pogues was felt in Terry Woods' 'Streets Of Sorrow' and Philip Chevron's classic anthem 'Thousands Are Sailing'. With its rich images of 'the old songs', 'fear of priest' and 'guilt and weeping effigies' the latter offered an imigrant's view of Ireland, but its dark undertones were counterbalanced by the unashamed sentiment of MacGowan's 'The Broad Majestic Shannon': 'I walked as day was dawning/ where small birds sang and leaves were falling/ where we once watched the row boats landing on the broad majestic Shannon.'

If 'The Broad Majestic Shannon' found solace in the past, then the preceding brace of bedtime stories were fashioned from its ghosts and spectres: with the lachrymose 'Lullaby Of London' providing a startling contrast to the dancing demons of 'Sit Down By The Fire'.

And although it was the accursed round of 'Birmingham Six' that echoed loudest, it was in the magical carousel of 'Medley' and the odds-on fervour of 'Bottle Of Smoke' that the full essence of 'Fall From Grace' was to be found.

As the LP shot straight to the top of the charts, The Pogues began a month-long tour of Australia and New Zealand, capturing an audience of 10,000 in Sydney alone, but managing to offend the natives as well as the Bi-centenary celebrating nationalists when one of the Australian stage crew unwittingly hung the Aborigine flag upside down.

Returning home, they released 'If I Should Fall From Grace With God' as a single and began a four-week trip around the country, under the appropriate dub 'Nobody Tells Me Anything'. The tour culminated in a week-long stint in London where, in front of a total audience of 17,000, they unveiled their greatest show yet.

Using the brass of their support stars After Tonite, The Pogues were able to pace the fierce momentum of 'Medley' and 'Sick Bed' with slow burners like 'A Rainy Night In Soho' and 'Fairytale Of New York'. Besides Kirsty MacColl, their guests included Joe Strummer, Steve Earle (singing 'Johnny Come Lately' with Spider), Mary Coughlan and Lynval Golding leading a cast of hundreds through 'A Message To You Rudi'.

With such luminaries sharing the spotlight, Shane was able to concentrate on playing bodhran as well as guitar, and – as they headed for their sixth year of live action – The Pogues were more of a unit than ever.

"We've all been very lucky that we weren't successful when we were younger," maintains Philip. "We've had 10 years or whatever to learn about ourselves as individuals and by and large we can take things in our stride. We're not arrogant little whippersnappers who've just had a gold record – we've got a combined age of 265, and that

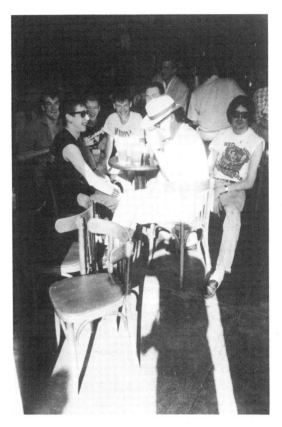

makes us very old indeed. It probably makes us older than any other group in the world bar The Chieftains and The Dubliners."

The Pogues might be on the verge of international phenomena, but the story so far is simply a vivid testimony to the power of chance, the magic of charisma and the importance of attitude.

discography

SINGLES

Dark Streets Of London/The Band Played Waltzing Matilda
Pogue Mahone Records PM1 (May 1984)

Dark Streets Of London/The Band Played Waltzing Matilda
Stiff BUY 207 (June 1984)

Boys From The County Hell/Repeal Of The Licensing Laws
Stiff BUY 212 (October 1984)

A Pair Of Brown Eyes/Whiskey You're The Devil
Stiff BUY 220 (March 1985)

A Pair Of Brown Eyes/Whiskey You're The Devil/Muirchin Dirkin
Stiff 12″ BUYIT 220 (March 1985)

Sally MacLennane/Wild Rover
Stiff BUY 224 (June 1985)

Sally MacLennane/Wild Rover/The Leaving Of Liverpool
Stiff 12″ BUYIT 224 (June 1985)

Dirty Old Town/A Pistol For Paddy Garcia
Stiff BUY 229 (August 1985)

Dirty Old Town/A Pistol For Paddy Garcia/The Parting Glass
Stiff 12″ BUYIT 229 (August 1985)

Haunted/Junk Theme
MCA 1084 (August 1986) (from the LP 'Sid & Nancy – Love Kills' MCA MCG 6011, July 1986, as entry below.)

Haunted/Junk Theme/Hot Dogs With Everything
MCA 12″ MCAT 1084 (August 1986)

The Irish Rover/The Rare Ould Mountain Dew
Stiff BUY 258 (March 1987) (with The Dubliners)

The Irish Rover/The Rare Ould Mountain Dew/The Dubliners Fancy
Stiff 12″ BUYIT 258 (March 1987) (with The Dubliners)

Fairytale Of New York/Battle March Medley
Pogue Mahone NY 7 (November 1987) (with Kirsty MacColl)

Fairytale Of New York/Battle March Medley/Shanne Bradley
Pogue Mahone 12″ NY12 (November 1987) (with Kirsty MacColl)

If I Should Fall From Grace With God/Sally MacLennane (live)
Pogue Mahone FG1 (February 1988)

If I Should Fall From Grace With God/Sally MacLennane (live)/A Pair Of Brown Eyes (live)
Pogue Mahone 12″ FG112 (February 1988)

Fiesta/Sketches Of Spain
Pogue Mahone FG2 (July 1988)

Fiesta/South Australia/Sketches Of Spain
Pogue Mahone 12″ FG212 (July 1988)

EXTENDED PLAYER

POGUETRY IN MOTION
London Girl/A Rainy Night In Soho/The Body Of An American Planxty/Noel Hill
Stiff BUY 243 (February 1986)
(Also available as 12″: Stiff BUYIT 243. The 7″ played at 33 rpm, the 12″ at 45 rpm.)

LONG PLAYERS

RED ROSES FOR ME
Transmetropolitan/The Battle Of Brisbane/The Auld Triangle/Waxies Dargle/Boys From The County Hell/Sea Shanty/Dark Streets Of London/Streams Of Whiskey/Poor Paddy/Dingle Regatta/Greenland Whale Fisheries/Down In The Ground Where The Dead Men Go/Kitty
Stiff SEEZ 55 (October 1984)

RUM, SODOMY AND THE LASH
The Sick Bed Of Cuchuliann/The Old Main Drag/Wild Cats Of Kilkenny/A Pair Of Brown Eyes/I'm A Man You Don't Meet Every Day/Sally MacLennane/Dirty Old Town/Jesse James/Billy's Bones/Navigator/The Gentleman Soldier/And The Band Played Waltzing Matilda
Stiff SEEZ 58 (August 1985)
(The CD and cassette versions of this LP also included A Pistol For Paddy Garcia)

STRAIGHT TO HELL: ORIGINAL SOUNDTRACK
The Good, The Bad And The Ugly/Rake At The Gates Of Hell/If I Should Fall From Grace With God/Rabinga/Danny Boy
Stiff DIABLO 1 (July 1987)
(This LP also features material by Joe Strummer, Steve Jones, Pray For Rain and Zander Schloss)

IF I SHOULD FALL FROM GRACE WITH GOD
If I Should Fall From Grace With God/Turkish Song Of The Damned/Bottle Of Smoke/Fairytale Of New York/Metropolis/Thousands Are Sailing/Fiesta/Medley: Recruiting Sergeant, Rocky Road To Dublin, Galway Races/Streets Of Sorrow/Birmingham Six/Lullaby Of London/Sit Down By The Fire/The Broad Majestic Shannon/Worms
Pogue Mahone NYR1 (January 1988)
(The CD version of this LP also included South Australia and The Battle March Medley)